THE QUALITY OF EXPRESSION

A Guide to Practical Criticism

David B. Strother
Washington State University

KENDALL/HUNT
PUBLISHING COMPANY
Dubuque, Iowa

Cover by Cheryl Strother

Library of Congress Catalog Card Number: 88-82236

ISBN 0–8403–4990–4

Printed in the United States of America
10 9 8 7 6 5 4 3 2

Contents

Preface   **vii**

CHAPTER 1   **Features of Quality in Expression   1**

A Model for Expression   **1**

Definitions of Quality   **2**

The Features of Quality   **3**

Feature One. Expression is of quality when understanding between two respondents is so intimate that the feelings, thoughts, and motives of one are readily incorporated by the other   **4**

Feature Two. Expression is of quality when it contains elements of unpredictability in composition and delivery   **5**

Feature Three. Expression is of quality when it is marked by a readiness to respond   **7**

Feature Four. Expression is of quality when it comes from the inner depths of the mind   **8**

Feature Five. Expression is of quality when it is motivated   **10**

Feature Six. Expression is of quality when it reflects goodness in the speaker   **12**

Feature Seven. Expression is of quality
when it leaves a lasting impression on
the listener   **13**

CHAPTER 2   The Elements of Expression   17

The Message   **17**
  Organizational Structure   **17**
  Amplification   **18**
  Emphasis   **18**
  Proportion   **19**
  Redundancy   **23**
The Speaker   **24**
  Trustworthiness   **25**
  Competence   **25**
  Dynamism   **25**
  Attractiveness   **25**
  Name Recognition   **26**
  Dress   **26**
  Similarity   **27**
The Audience   **27**
Channels   **28**
The Occasion   **29**

CHAPTER 3   The Criticism of Speeches   31

Forms of Communication Events   **31**
What Is Criticism?   **32**
Why Engage in Criticism?   **32**
Types of Criticism   **33**
The Critical Method: Speeches You Witness   **34**
The Critical Method: Speeches You Read   **41**

APPENDIX 1   Recognizing Misused Vocal Cues   47

APPENDIX 2   **Speeches for Analysis**   **51**

John Forbes Kerry
Testimony Before the Committee on
    Foreign Relations, United States Senate
April 22, 1971   **51**

Analysis

Ronald Reagan
"We Dare to Hope for our Children"
July 3, 1986   **61**

Michele Nilsen
"Are You Fit for Life?"
March 20, 1986   **65**

Brenda W. Simonson
"Corporate Fitness Programs Pay Off"
May 19, 1986   **69**

Gerry Sikorski
"Will and Vision"
June 1, 1986   **75**

Ichiro Hattori
"Trade Conflicts"
November 19, 1985   **83**

Index   **91**

Preface

An incident recently occurred in one of my classes that convinced me of an urgent need for a book of this kind. A student had just completed a four-minute speech, and with all due respect to the student it was rather mediocre. I was unable to find those elements which supposedly combine to create a verbally logical speech—unity, coherence, and emphasis. In addition, he made no perceptible attempt to adapt himself or his subject matter to his audience. Upon sitting down, a member of the class stated most assertively, "That was a great speech and I think the speaker deserves an 'A'." Whatever the motive for such a comment, it was ill-chosen and it revealed a naivete possessed not simply by this one individual but undoubtedly by many of his peers. It indicates to me that (1) many students seem content to accept a mediocre speech as something worthy of praise largely because (2) they lack the analytical skills necessary to discern quality from mediocrity in expression.

Unfortunately, this is a common phenomenon not only with students but with the public at large who appear to tolerate mediocrity as the norm. In retrospect, I, too, lacked those critical instincts as an instructor teaching his first college class in public speaking. I had learned well the rules of effective communication, but after first hearing a group of student speeches and collecting their outlines, I sat down and said to myself, "What should I be looking for? Where should I be focusing my comments?" I could correct the outlines according to the rules in the text and write a smorgasbord of reactions about their presentational styles, but there appeared to be no system to what I was doing and there was certainly no assurance that the next presentations would be any more effective. After years of similar quandaries with student speeches, it occurred to me that if I could critique the effects of students' speeches with the same informed intensity as I use when instructing them about how to put a speech together and deliver it effectively, then three goals could be accomplished: (1) students would develop informed insights into what makes for effective speaking; (2) they would have a systematic and informed method available to them to analyze the effects of others' speeches; and (3) they could discern certain unique attributes each speaker possessed for better or for worse.

Virtually every public speaking text currently on the market provides the necessary instruction and exercises to assist in achieving the first two goals. The authors have clearly and meticulously set forth instructions based on proven rhetorical principles which comprise "good" oral communication. It is likely, also, that students' speech grades are based on the degree to which they employed a selected set of those principles. That is well and good as far as it goes, but it is also a real possibility that the criticism may be cosmetic and fail to get to root causes for speeches that simply fall flat. Perhaps if one more item were added to each assignment—the degree to which those universally recognized rhetorical principles are reflected in a few well-defined behavioral features unique to quality expression—then maybe all three of the goals could be more effectively achieved. With that idea in mind, the purpose of this book is to suggest an approach to criticism which might serve to stimulate thought about the way we criticize speech performance. I have chosen to propose a method for diagnosis rather than prescription.

As yet, this has been attempted in very few instances. The best treatment of criticism, in my judgment, currently available is book titled, *A Choice of Worlds,* by James A. Andrews. In it Professor Andrews focuses on six principles the critic should examine when looking at speeches as literature. He then provides a sample public speech with an analysis emphasizing one principle in each speech. The book is valuable, but its scope is limited.

Having established the purpose for this book, I want to prepare you for what follows. It is intended to supplement the basic text which will set forth the rhetorical principles. After the student has a reasonable handle on those principles, this book may then come into use to help explain some of the things which happen during rhetorical transactions that are the result of individual behaviors.

The plan of this book is simple, consisting of three parts. First, I attempt to bring to the readers' consciousness unique features underlying quality expression. Second, I provide places in the elements of communication where critics might look for them. Last of all, I suggest means by which those discoveries might be communicated. I want this book to be a guide to practical assessment. If it helps a little, then perhaps its birth has not been in vain.

David Strother

1

Features of Quality in Expression

In this chapter, you are introduced to the natural features which largely comprise quality of expression in all communicative situations—formal, as in public speaking, or informal as in conversations or small group activities; in person, where you can observe and be observed, or *not* in-person where you observe a speaker on television but *not* be observed, or when you read a speech recorded long after it was delivered. These forces will subsequently serve as guidelines for you to appraise the degree of quality in all expression which involves you as a participant.

A Model for Expression

In this book, the author has selected the conversational model as the foundation for expression. Upon close scrutiny, you will find it compatible with the model presented in your text. Two people conversing on a park bench may be considered as two respondents (R^1-R^2). Each is reacting simultaneously to the other. Only one may be verbally reacting, but the other is surely reacting nonverbally. Each is sending the other messages received through the senses, weighed against past experiences and beliefs, and reacted to verbally or nonverbally. The conversation is sustained when one is able to identify, relate, or share his or her past experiences and beliefs with those of the other. The closer the identification, the more enjoyable the conversation.

With the conversational model in mind, you are seated in an auditorium with a speaker at the podium. You are still in an R^1–R^2 situation only certain social constraints are present. The speaker is reacting verbally and you are reacting nonverbally. You are still looking for the opportunity to share past experiences and beliefs. When that opportunity presents itself, you send that cue nonverbally to the speaker who, in turn, pleased by your response, feeds you more of the same. In the formal or public speaking situation you are conversing in much the same way that you conversed on the park bench except for the social constraints. Obviously, those constraints can introduce problems or *noise* reducing the mutual sharing of past experiences and beliefs. For example, the speaker may incorrectly read your responsive cues and continue blithely on a course which ultimately produces dissociation between the two of you.

Always keep in mid the conversational model as you read this book, and when you run across terms like *speaker*, *listener*, and *audience*, relate them to the model.

Definition of Quality

Among several definitions you might encounter, two stand out as having significance. *First, quality is the degree of excellence.* Although that definition is very general, it tends to focus on excellence, and that is your concern. For purposes of this book, quality will mean having reached that pinnacle of communicative effectiveness. A second definition comes from Robert Pirsig's contemporary Phaedrus who, while instructing a college class, wrote on the board this definition: "Quality is a characteristic of thought and statement that is recognized by a nonthinking process. Because definitions are a product of rigid, formal thinking, quality cannot be defined." While Phaedrus has to admit ignorance about quality, he recovered sufficiently to write beneath that definition, "But even though quality cannot be defined, you know what quality is."[1] So, *quality in expression is the product of impressions which move two respondents closer together in thoughts and actions.*

2

You can easily discern pleasurable conversation from boring or tedious conversation. You have had such moments where time stood still; where you were so drawn to that other person that you were unaware of the presence of others; where distance was but an abstraction; where the symbiosis between the two of you was so strong that the universe was composed of two people—you and your friend. You can also discern a "good" public speech from a boring one, though perhaps not as easily because the communication appears on the surface so one-sided. In retrospect, whenever you are so attentive to a speaker that you are momentarily unaware of the presence of anyone else around you, you are likely listening to a "good" public speech.

Now, look at some of the causes which produced those inner feelings, and in so doing, you are starting your journey through that wonderful, yet complex, abstraction called *quality*. Remember, for purposes of this book, whenever the word, quality, is used it will be understood to mean excellence in communication.

The Features of Quality

Explaining quality in expression may be compared to explaining the growth system of a tree. There is first the root system which is the heart and soul of the tree. We are not often attentive to it or the directions of its roots, but we know that without it, there would be no tree. Then there is the trunk with thick, broad branches at the base and thinner branches as we scan toward the top. They comprise the elements of expression. Along each branch are even smaller branches clothed with leaves. These are words, phrases, and mannerisms most readily observable in expression. As we move closer to the tree we develop a better understanding of the relationship of the part to the whole. As we step back with ever increasing distance, the trunk becomes smaller, the branches become hidden by the leaves, and we view a single artifact of nature in all of its stunning beauty and

3

majesty made possible by the natural unity of all of its parts unseen and uncomprehended from a distance.

Expression, too, has its root system which, like the tree, may well serve as its heart and soul. You do not at first train your eyes on it because you are observing its end product— words, phrases, and mannerisms. Nevertheless, the root system each of us possesses consists of seven basic features which, in turn, serves as the basis for quality in all human communication.

FEATURE ONE

Expression is of quality when understanding between two respondents is so intimate that the feelings, thoughts, and motives of one are readily incorporated by the other.

Two minds become totally immersed as one, and as the two of you begin to think alike you begin to act alike, as well. For example, two people attentive to an idea will display similar physical reactions to that idea. Another term for this phenomenon is _empathy_. In the arts, particularly theatre, the message of the playwright is conveyed to an audience through characters, plot, and scenery, and the message becomes credible when we react in tandem with the characters. When they cry and we in turn are saddened, then the empathic response is at work. In informal conversation, when one respondent expresses certain feelings he or she has lived through and when the other respondent also experiences those feelings, empathy is at work. In more formalized situations, call them public speaking situations, the same holds true, but is more difficult to achieve.

This first principle, if you can achieve it, will assure you of quality in your expression. But what if you do not? There is still hope by moving on to the other principles.

Example. James L. Kilpatrick, a noted columnist, once remarked that of the 10,000 speeches he must have heard, the greatest of those was delivered by Charles Malik, former ambassador to the United Nations from Lebanon.[2] As he presented the speech in Williamsburg, Virginia, on June 11, 1960, Malik "held a tough audience absolutely spellbound for 57 minutes."

Explanation. What about the other 9,999 speeches? Kilpatrick dismisses them with this comment: "Once upon a time we had orators who could move men by the sheer power of spoken words. . . . Where are such golden voices now?"

Reaction. On the national scene, there are a few "golden voices" around but the odds of our being recipients of their eloquence are remote. On the private scene, particularly in informal communicative situations, we have all most likely been recipients.

FEATURE TWO

Expression is of quality when it contains elements of unpredictability in composition and delivery.

Writing in *Scientific American*, Woodburn Heron, points out some of the effects of prolonged exposure to a monotonous environment.[3] He alludes to a study for the Royal Air Force during WWII to find out why radar operators on anti-submarine patrol sometimes failed to detect U-boats. The operators usually worked in isolation, watching a radar screen hour after hour. The researchers set up a comparable laboratory situation requiring subjects to watch a pointer moving around a graduated dial and to press a button whenever the pointer made a double jump. The subjects' efficiency declined in the surprisingly short time of half an hour. Heron has also observed that even invertebrates respond in a similar fashion. If you shake the surface on which a snail is resting, it withdraws into its shell. If you shake it repeatedly, the snail after a while fails to react.

Monotony, then, that wearisome sameness which lulls minds into somnolence, becomes a potential hazard to quality expression., In communication, monotony is not usually isolated to one behavioral manifestation, but occurs in concert with other behavioral cues. For example, if vocal variation is limited to a very narrow range, it is likely that bodily response is also confined to very narrow limits. This response usually occurs when one relies excessively on notes. And the narrower the limits, the greater the degree of predictability.

While unpredictability through the expression of thought and action is most desirable, *your unpredictable manner must never be threatening to other respondents.* One who precipitously wads-up notes, hurls them across the room, and jumps-up on a desk gesticulating wildly while shouting incoherently exhibits behavior which is threatening to those present and violates their sense of safety.

> **Example.** A student once began a speech by placing a chair on top of a desk, sat in the chair and began shouting: "Hey, quit throwing sand! Don't you dare go in that water! You are too far out, get back in here!"

> **Explanation.** She was dramatizing her summer job as a life guard. After that introduction, she got off the desk and began communicating in an acceptable manner.

> **Reaction.** Her starting behavior was shockingly unusual. For a few moments we had to weight the safety factor in view of this highly unpredictable behavior. We finally decided we were safe. Unfortunately, we tended to remain preoccupied with the trauma of the introduction and giving less attention to her subsequent remarks.

> **Example.** The author was once lecturing on patterns of outlining when a normally subdued member of the

6

class raised his hand. When recognized, he said, "It has occurred to me that we have abandoned the Jeffersonian principles of democracy."

Explanation. The student was a veteran of the Korean war who had been badly wounded to where doctors implanted a steel plate in his head to replace a portion of the skull.

Reaction. The student's reaction was so incongruous to the discussion at hand, that the author became very uneasy for the remainder of the class period for fear the student might seriously disrupt the proceedings.

FEATURE THREE

Expression is a quality when it is marked by a readiness to respond.

By the term, "readiness to respond," is meant (1) the attention the speaker gives to his or her subject during its preparation and delivery, and (2) the attention the speaker gives to audience cues readily enabling him or her to adapt to the changing moods of the audience. In the act of preparation, a speaker may develop a readiness to respond by use of inquiry into the topic. The question would be a good example. As you prepare a speech, ask questions like, "What if I were to go in this direction for my next point; or Should I relate a personal experience here?" By use of questions and answers, you sharpen the mind so that it is reasonably prepared to respond to the ideas you have internally generated. In the act of delivery, you tend to communicate in declarative idea groupings, and you do that in two ways: (1) by verbal means, and (2) by nonverbal means. Normally, when you are declarative, you are presenting yourself as an authority on whatever the idea is that you have just asserted. If you say, "It is a beautiful day," you are declaratively verbalizing with nonverbal accoutrements. If you care about your credibility as a com-

7

municator, you should believe you have adequate reasons for saying what you say. In short, be an expert on what you assert to be true.

This admonition holds true in any communicative situation, but assume for the moment that you have a formal speech to present to a group. Select a topic that you know in depth. Then take a small segment of that topic and discuss it in detail. Explaining smaller components of a topic provokes your mind to focus on them with a greater degree of sharpness. You are readily responding. This is much more desirable than were you to confine your remarks to broad generalities which in themselves lull the mind into a sluggish state. As a consequence, your total outward responsiveness will reflect the inner action of your mind.

So far we have talked about readiness to respond to a topic. Now we need to discuss a speaker's readiness to respond to others. Since you have selected a topic that you are knowledgeable about, and you have narrowed it so that you can develop it in detail, you must develop the sensitivity to respond to audience inquiry. In formalized situations that inquiry will most likely come to you nonverbally through facial expression and other physical cues. You must read that response and react to it. A quizzical look might suggest that you have given too vague an explanation for something, In that event, having read that reaction, you are inclined to say something like, "I see too many quizzical looks, so let me go through this process a bit more slowly." If you do this, you are showing a readiness to respond to your topic and to your audience.

FEATURE FOUR

Expression is of quality when it comes from the inner depths of the mind.

Picture your thought process as consisting of two layers—an outer layer requiring little energy to reveal what

8

is there, and an inner layer requiring a relatively large expenditure of energy as you probe its depths. For example, it requires far less concentration and energy to observe that it is a beautiful day than were you to bring to the surface all of the conscious observations which led you to your original conclusion. To say, "It is a beautiful day," is a reaction requiring little thought and little energy. In short, it is a generalization, and a generalization by its very nature is abstract; it does not create imagery or excite because it is without reference to a specific instance to stimulate you or your respondent to be attentive.

Realistically, all communication has within it abstraction. Although it cannot be avoided, it can be placed where it serves definite purposes. For example, in formal speaking situations, the authors of your text probably discuss the importance of previewing and summarizing the main ideas you want to bring forth. Those are abstractions and possess inherently the shortcomings discussed above. But they are a necessary prelude to the in-depth development of ideas which comprises the sum and substance of the speech. Other examples of constructive abstraction occur in informal communicative situations because, initially, it is your way of adjusting socially to another person. If you are with this person for a protracted period of time, however, your conversation gradually gravitates into the inner layers of both your mind and that of the respondent. Conversation, then, or even formal speaking evolves into an intriguing experience because it opens the door for (1) empathic responses, (2) unpredictable, yet comfortable, exchanges of ideas and behaviors, and (3) a readiness to respond.

Example. There is a theory called the "starving artist" theory which declares that during the act of creating art, the artist endures deprivation in order to keep mind and body focused on the creative endeavor. Too many interruptions would disturb the depth of concentration. Thomas Edison, the inventor, supposedly deprived

9

himself of sleep so as not to disturb his thought processes.

Explanation. People react differently when they are in process of "inventing" a formal speech. Some like to put a speech together at one time employing whatever depth of concentration is necessary to complete the task. The only difficulty is that the longer one expends energy in concentration, the less efficient one becomes in probing the depths of the mind for suitable compelling information. Others like to put a speech together over time, jotting notes when a good idea strikes them. Then, a day or two before speaking, they synthesize the material they have collected in a relatively short period of time.

Reaction. The author recommends the latter method. Useful ideas normally need a period of incubation. They seldom appear in a moment of inspiration.

FEATURE FIVE

Expression is of quality when it is motivated.

It is far better to speak because you want to, not because you have to. On the stage, an actor is motivated to perform because of the challenge of conveying to a fresh audience the believability of the character being portrayed. In conversation, you may be motivated to contribute because you have an idea you really want to toss into the communication hopper, or because you simply want to react in a favorable manner hoping your respondent will think better of you. In the classroom you speak on a given day because you have been assigned that day. You *have* to speak. On the surface, it would appear as if you are caught in a trap. How can you be motivated to speak if you have to? You do it the same way an actor would who portrays the same character night after night. The difference is that you are conveying a meaningful idea about which you are an expert and, through preparation, you have developed a readiness to respond to the ideas you have generated. Now, your are ready to share them with others, for through sharing, you enjoy the wonders of interaction that you have experienced many times before in informal communication.

At this juncture, you may ask how you will know when the speaker is motivated? The simplest answer is, you will know! In a figurative sense, there will be electricity in the room perpetually generated through mutually understood and mutually shared behavioral cues. In a literal sense, the speaker will be physically alert and direct as if prepared to instantly respond to any cue he or she observes.

As a listener, how might you be expected to react? You will not know it at the time, but if you are truly sharing ideas with the speaker, your behavior will be similar—you will have the symptoms of behavioral alertness and directness.

> **Example**. The author, at one time an avid coin collector, was chatting before class with two students about the twenty dollar gold coin once minted in the United States. The conversation was very intense. As other students filed into the room, the initial intensity spread throughout until it permeated the entire class. Their behavioral response indicated that they wanted to hear more, and the author was more than happy to oblige. Later, much to his consternation, the major portion of class time had been consumed much to the surprise of everyone present.

> **Explanation**. The author was motivated to talk about a subject which had great interest to him. The students were motivated to want to hear more about a coin which carried with it a mystique of Americana.

> **Reaction**. The lesson plan for that day had to be postponed, but in its place came a real life example of the pleasure of motivated expression.

You, as a respondent, require that a person with whom you are communicating exude an aura of goodness. It shows itself through the two major factors of safety and expertise, and various other factors such as dynamism, attractiveness, name recognition, and similarity, among other considerations discussed by scholars in the field of persuasion.

You feel safe not only when a speaker is non-threatening, but when he or she displays traits of congeniality, calmness, patience, and fairness. You also require the speaker to have expertise on the subject under discussion as it might be reflected by experience, training, intelligence, and authoritativeness.

Among other factors mentioned above are characteristics of credibility which, depending on the circumstances, can have powerful persuasive influence. The first is *dynamism* or the forcefulness of a speaker's presentation. It may be characterized by much large muscle movement as in walking about or gesturing, and is often accompanied by the speaker's use of humor. *Attractiveness* is another strong factor in credibility. Robert Cialdini cites a number of studies which indicate that a physically attractive person evinces persuasion more effectively than one with "ordinary" features.[4] Erwin Bettinghaus, a scholar of persuasion, points out that "goodlooking people are perceived to be more likeable, friendly, interesting, and poised . . . more likely to be successful, to make more money, and so on."[5] *Name recognition* also carries strong persuasive effect. It is not uncommon for a celebrities to to promote various products because they are accepted for their credibility. *Dress* is another important variable. It tells us about the degree of respect the speaker has for himself or herself and the audience. And last of all, *similarity*, may be a strong force in credibility. People tend to accept as credible those who display characteristics they feature themselves as having.

If you believe what someone tells you, it is a virtual certainty that person possesses several of of the elements of credibility mentioned above.

FEATURE SEVEN

Expression is of quality when it leaves a lasting impression on the listener.

So much of what guides our lives today have come to us from memorable impressions left by parents, relatives, friends, teachers, and to a lesser degree, public speakers whose words have left an indelible niche in our minds. They may consist of isolated phrases, but they, nevertheless, become a part of ourselves and they emerge from time to time into our consciousness still possessed with a power to influence our daily lives.

The bombing of Pearl Harbor is but a page of history to many of you, but to this author, even at the age of twelve, I remember vividly the events of the following day. Around noon, the principle of the junior high school assembled all of the seventh and eighth graders in a makeshift auditorium with nothing on the stage except for a radio resting on top of a chair. We then heard President Franklin Roosevelt address a joint session of Congress. He reviewed the events of the previous day and concluded by resolutely declaring that a state of war exists between the United States and the Imperial government of Japan. As distasteful as war is, that rhetorical act of the President did as much to unite the American people as the bombing itself could possibly have done.

"I have been to the mountain and I have seen the promised land . . . ," is an excerpt taken from Martin Luther King's last speech that still holds great meaning because we all have mountains to climb and there may be that one which will give us a view of good things to come. Each of us has a memory bank of phrases, mottos, and stories which have come to us through moments of memorable communication.

> **Example.** A student recently began her speech with a touching story about how she was losing her hair. She then related the advice she had received from her dermatologist about the causes and cures for such a condition.

> **Reaction.** The audience was very attentive. The author "took the cure" and to this day owes a dept of gratitude to that young lady.

Summary

You have been introduced to the seven features comprising the root system of criticism. You know that expression is of quality when:

1. Understanding between two respondents is so intimite that the feelings, thoughts, and motives of one are readily incorporated by the other.
2. It contains elements of unpredictability in composition and delivery.
3. It is marked by a readiness to respond.
4. It comes from the inner depths of the mind.
5. It is motivated.
6. It reflects goodness in the speaker.
7. It leaves a lasting impression on the listener.

They now conjoin to form a broad and sturdy trunk with large branches leading from it. Those branches are the second most important consideration in our quest to locate the components of expression.

Footnotes (Chapter 1)

1. Robert M. Persig, *Zen and the Art of Motorcycle Maintenance* (New York: Bantam Books, 1974), pp. 200–203.
2. James L. Kilpatrick, ''Where have all the speakers gone,'' *Daily Idahonian,* July 28, 1980, p. 4.
3. Woodburn Heron, ''The Pathology of Boredom,'' *Scientific American,* vol. 196 (1957), pp. 52–56.
4. Robert B. Cialdini, *Influence: Science and Practice.* 2nd ed. (Glenview, Ill.: Scott, Foresman and Company, 1988), pp. 161–163.
5. Erwin Bettinghaus and Michael J. Cody, *Persuasive Communication.* 4th ed. (New York: Holt, Rinehart and Winston, 1987) p. 94.

The Elements of Expression

The Message

An effective message will contain (1) organizational structure; (2) amplification; (3) emphasis; (4) proportion; and (5) redundancy.

Organizational Structure

Virtually all speech is built around some kind of a framework whether you are engaged in casual conversation or giving a formal speech. In the first instance, that framework may not be apparent because you are exchanging short, concise utterances with another person while fully anticipating responses which may take you in directions you could not plan. In formal speaking, logical verbal order is particularly important for three reasons: (1) because of the absence of verbal response, you must chart for your listeners a clear progression of idea development so there is no confusion about where you are taking them, (2) a well-structured speech will enhance their perception of your competence, and (3) studies indicate that listeners prefer some kind of organizational structure. Whether the organization is loose as in conversation or tightly structured as in formal speaking, it is the substance which gives what you say a semblance of logical verbal order commonly known as unity, coherence, and emphasis. The chapter(s) in your text will illustrate in detail how you go about organizing a speech.

Amplification

When a speaker amplifies, he or she provides the outer cover for the framework of organization. Amplification is explanation through examples, descriptions, definitions, comparisons, testimonies, and statistics. In a large measure, it makes an utterance compelling by providing verbal images which capture the respondent's attention, much like what an incident on television seeks to do, causing the respondent to experience the same mental and emotional behavior as the speaker. It was referred to earlier as the empathic response. See Feature One.

Emphasis

While relegated under the message, emphasis is so important that it could easily be placed in a separate category by itself because it provides a point of focus for communication to really take place. To illustrate, the author recently paid a visit to the Rijksmuseum in Amsterdam where paintings of the great Dutch masters were on exhibit. Upon entering one large room where a large painting adorned each of its four walls, his eyes were soon drawn to one painting in particular. It was Rembrandt's, "The Night Watchman." While each painting was a masterpiece in its detail, "The Night Watchman" really stood out for reasons later explained by the guide. Rembrandt had used light to move the observers' eyes to a particular point of action in the painting itself. In this painting and others, he commanded that people view what he wanted them to view. The other Dutch masters had provided no such points of focus. As masterful as the detail was in their paintings, the observer had to supply the focus which possessed no particular significance.

Verbal Emphasis. Communication becomes much more meaningful when you supply focus for the respondent through emphasis. There are two kinds of emphasis, verbal and nonverbal. Certain forms of verbal emphasis have been shown to be very effective in terms of aiding a respondent's retention of a message. In an experiment conducted by Ray Ehrensberger, there were significant differences between speeches containing the following forms of verbal emphasis and the same speeches which did not include emphasis.[1] They are listed here in order of importance.

1. Verbal emphasis ("Now get this," prior to the remark).
2. Three distributed repetitions (at the beginning, in the middle, at the end).
3. Immediate repetitions early in the speech.
4. Speaking slowly (half the normal rate)
5. Immediate repetitions late in the speech.

In addition to helping the respondent grab and retain selected ideas, often the speaker's use of these verbal "signposts" prompts his or her readiness to respond. See Feature Three.

Nonverbal Emphasis. The second form of emphasis is nonverbal which may be divided into (1) physical response, and (2) vocal response which includes (a) loudness, (b) melody or variations of pitch, and (c) time and its constituents—the pause, duration or the prolongation of sounds, and the speed of one's speech, and (d) vocal quality (see Appendix 1). Use of these codes can give added impetus to important ideas. Ehrensberger noted two of them as having significant effects:

6. Pauses.
7. Gestures (hand and index finger only).

While effective and timely use of these nonverbal components enhances the quality of expression, they are among the most difficult rhetorical devices to acquire because you may not have been taught to use them and you habitually do not. Sometimes they will spontaneously manifest themselves when the speaker reaches certain extremes of emotions like anger or happiness.

Proportion

Proportion plays a large role in the message. By proportion is meant the relative importance you place in the amplification of an idea. Some ideas need to be developed proportionately more than others because of their complexity. Others because they are more important. Still others because the audience is obviously captivated and wants to hear more. In this section, there are three considerations: (1) the importance of where to place ideas and adapt them to audience cues; (2) the role energy plays in proportion; and (3) the importance of masking or de-emphasis.

1) *Where to place ideas.* While literature in persuasion abounds with reserved admonitions about where to place your most important ideas—whether at the beginning or at the end of a speech, they seem to all agree that you should never place them in the middle. As a general rule, in the course of preparation, this author recommends that you place them at the beginning with the most important idea first followed by the next most important. Why? Because listening requires a degree of concentration, concentration requires energy, and the energy level of listeners is likely to be higher at the beginning of a speech than at the end. Later, as one develops sensitivity to communication, he or she can then sense where, when, and how to regulate that energy flow.

During the presentation of a speech, be prepared to adapt to thoughts which spontaneously pop into your mind and which seem to belong naturally to the development of your subject matter. Also be mindful of the messages being communicated to you by your respondents. There may well be certain ideas they will want you to amplify further for clarification or simply for pure enjoyment. These are points in a speech where a readiness to respond is vital for quality communication. Often speakers comment that they are unable to read their audience's responses and are therefore unable to adapt. In reply, remember, individual responses are there just as they are in conversation. Select one, two, or three people at random and answer their concerns. If their responses are so subtle you cannot get an accurate reading, then you can elicit an even more overt response by asking a question like, "Can you follow what I am saying?" Or, you can bait response with statements like, "Let me give you another example," or "Let me see if I can state this idea another way."

The role of energy in proportion. In communication levels of energy are constantly being conveyed and received between respondents. The proportionate use of that energy determines the relative effectiveness of a message. By energy is meant the behavioral manifestation of mental and overt physical responses. Examples of mental energy may consist of compelling stories, apt quotations, picturesque language, and examples and illustrations as mentioned earlier. Examples of physical energy are vocal force, crisp articulation, large muscle movement, and penetrating eye contact. They will occur in varying degrees from weak to intense, but the purposeful use of that energy determines how compelling a message will be. For example, if two people read an identical piece of literature they will read it differently, and you will likely prefer one rendition over another because the energy output of one reader tends to draw you into the reading more effectively than the energy output of the other.

The effective use of that energy falls somewhere between what Melvin Rader and Bertram Jessup call "creative intent and appreciative response that makes the work of art a living thing."[2] The graph below illustrates what happens and why to the energy flow in the course of a hypothetical speech. Assume the speaker is presenting three reasons why one should buy mutual funds.

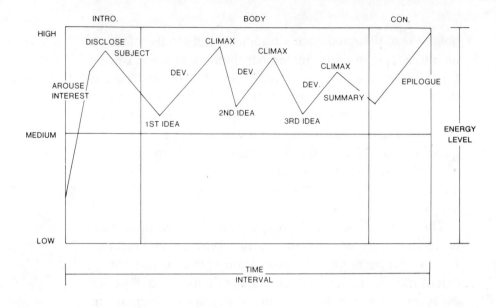

At the very beginning, the energy level is relatively low because the first words are simply form words to help build imagery for the rest of the attention arouser. Now the energy level builds with the mental exercise being used to form images from the language being conveyed. Also there is a noticeable acceleration of physical energy. When the subject is revealed, it is necessarily generalized which produces a decline in energy output—it leaves nothing to the imagination. As the speaker amplifies or develops the generalization, the energy level increases in intensity because the mental process of the respondents is at work identifying or relating the material to their reference frames. When the second reason is stated, the energy level again will begin its ascent as additional supporting material is introduced and as identification, once again, takes place. Only this time the energy level does not peak quite as high as with the first point because fatigue begins to eat-away at attentiveness. At the conclusion of the second point, energy drops with the introduction of the third point. This time our energy output peaks at an even lower level than with the second point. Fatigue continues to take its toll. At the conclusion, energy drops again but soon rises with the speaker's epilogue—a telling climax to the entire speech. It is the final sprint to the finish line. When all is said, the respondent is left with an active mind and body, until the final let down—behavioral proof that quality through proportion was at work during the speech.

Masking or de-emphasis. While effective communicators use emphasis to drive-home important points or to otherwise heighten positive features in their presentations, they also use masking to disguise or de-emphasize weaknesses which might have a detrimental effect on their communication. Kenneth Burke uses the term "trained incapacity." For example, if a speaker's physical movements are awkward or distracting, he or she may reduce those movements and compensate with compelling supporting material. The opposite may hold true, as well. If the speaker's supporting material is weak or appears to lack compellingness, he or she may seek to compensate with a greater degree of physical energy. Accomplished communicators know their strengths and weaknesses.

Redundancy

Most likely all quality communication will contain the feature of redundancy. It is analogous to back-up systems on complicated mechanical devices. In oral communication, redundancy is the subtle and sometimes not so subtle way of reminding respondents what they may have missed earlier. Because oral communication, particularly, relies on instant intelligibility, it needs back-up systems so if a respondent missed an idea on the first round, there will be other opportunities to pick it up later. Television soap operas are replete with redundancy because the writers of those programs work on the assumption that a significantly large number of viewers miss installments from time to time and redundancy fills them in on what they missed. Emphasis through verbal repetition is one of those desirable, yet not so subtle forms of redundance. Restatement is another form and is a trifle more subtle.

Redundancy is not only necessary for the respondent, it is necessary for the speaker as well. It serves as a reminder of what has been covered and what yet needs to be covered. It is a way of nurturing that readiness to respond which will, in turn, add a liveliness and an unpredictability to the communication. See Feature Two.

Of course redundancy can be overworked, but in the classroom it seldom is for several reasons: (1) many students believe that word-for-word repetition of an idea is unnecessary, therefore they do not do it; (2) many students do not have that responsive readiness which would enable them to express the idea in different words; and (3) many students are either using manuscripts or they have rehearsed their speeches to a point where they can perform them mechanically without ever having to explore the inner depths of their minds while speaking.

The Speaker

Although placed in separate categories, you really cannot completely separate the message from the speaker. After all, the message is the brainchild of the speaker and his or her persona is intricately intertwined with the verbal substance of the message. There are, however, other elements in the speaker's persona which can and should be treated separately.

The speaker must, above all, be believable. A portion of that believability will come from the impact of the message which we have already discussed. The remainder of believability will come from the degree of credibility he or she establishes with you. In Principle Six, there were six components which comprise believability in a speaker:

trustworthiness, competence, dynamism, attractiveness, name recognition, dress, and similarity.

Trustworthiness

According to a study by Berlo, Lemert, and Mertz, when a speaker is perceived to be trustworthy he or she ranks high as one who is kind, gentle, congenial, warm, agreeable, pleasant, unselfish, forgiving, fair, sociable, patient, and calm.[3] Because of these positive traits, you may on occasion overlook any deficiencies he or she may possess as an expert in a particular field.

Competence

There are occasions, though, where you may want an expert or at least someone you consider competent by virtue of known skills, experience, training, or general intelligence. In a speaking situation, you often will judge the competence of a classmate on the basis of the way he or she puts a message together. Is it skillfully organized? Does the speaker draw on the experiences of authorities in the field actually mentioning them by name and by source? Are the ideas explained in a clear manner?

Dynamism

Dynamism is another feature of speaker credibility often cited in the literature on persuasion. By dynamism is meant a lot of physical movement, mental alertness or that readiness to respond, penetrating eye contact, and a strong vocal responsiveness. They are compelling behaviors which have the potential of creating a mental and physical alertness in audience members.

Attractiveness

A fourth variable in speaker credibility is attractiveness. This is perhaps a more powerful persuasive influence than many are led to believe. Numerous studies cited by Cialdini suggest that attractive people seem to appear favored. But for those of us in the world who are ugly, take heart! John

Wilkes, an eighteenth century member of Parliament in Great Britain who was considered to be a very ugly man, is reported to have said that he could talk away his face, and be only a "quarter behind the handsomest man." This is not to imply that less attractive people play "second banana," but it suggests that speakers with less favorable physical attributes had better develop other strengths in their personas and in the preparation and delivery of their messages.

Name Recognition

Name recognition is another factor in credibility. This is the reason sports, movie, and television stars are hired at handsome fees to promote products. This may also be a reason for possibly acceding to opinions expressed by peers who have the reputation of being leaders. Closely related to name recognition is status differentiation. You are likely to accept ideas advanced by professors over graduate teaching assistants if given the opportunity to compare; you will likely accept the opinions of your congressional representative over that of your political science instructor; you will likely take to heart the admonitions on how to become a better public speaker expressed by a popular local television personality than by your professor seated in the room wearing a tattered sport coat.

Dress

That last example brings to mind the importance of dress in establishing credibility. As a general rule, dress should be appropriate to the occasion. A speaker should dress neatly, but not in such a manner that it would distract. Neat attire, selected with discretion, is a sign of cultivation or good taste—an admirable quality in any speaker. A friend of the author who had recently retired and was arranging to move from the area, clothed himself regularly in a suit and tie because the attire won him immediate attention and service at various agencies with whom he had to make arrangements.

Similarity

Similarity is the final variable in speaker credibility. This concept simply says that people prefer others who are similar to themselves, particularly if they have good feelings about themselves. If a person likes what you like, the similarity produces closeness; if a person behaves in a manner similar to the way you think you behave, you are drawn closer to that person; if a person expresses beliefs somewhat similar to yours, you like that person.

The Audience

When Aristotle wrote *The Rhetoric*, he devoted an entire book to consideration of the audience including demographics and consideration of various emotions. He did so because he knew that orators, to be persuasive, had to adapt their messages to meet the needs of their listeners. The same holds true today. With recent findings in the literature of psychology, sociology, and communication, the speaker has a much better opportunity to analyze audiences and adapt messages to them with a higher degree of accuracy than ever before. Roderick P. Hart and Don M. Burks have a term for this kind of assessment called *rhetorical sensitivity*.[4] The effects of this sensitivity appear particularly in Features One and Three.

Since the purpose of this chapter is to give you ideas about what constitutes quality in speaking, the author will not go into a study of the audience, per se, since we are looking at communication from the view of *you*, the observer. In so doing, you may use one or both of two approaches. In the first approach, you may view a speech as a detached, impersonal observer seeking behavioral data from the presentation which attests to its degree of technical accuracy. Likely, you will seek answers to questions like, "Did the Introduction accomplish its purpose; What pattern of organization was used in the Body; Did the speaker maintain eye contact?" And so on. If you can be fully attentive to these considerations while one is speaking, chances are the speech was *not* one of quality because you did not permit the speaker to engage you in a truly responsive communicative situation. In the second approach, you are concerned less with analyzing the speaker, but simply letting yourself be a member of the audience. Your analysis will occur only after the speaker has concluded. You then can begin your analysis with a post communication general observation like, "I really liked that speech." Then you devote your analysis to looking for the reasons.

While you play a key role as "audience," this does not mean to imply that you cannot be influenced by those around you if there are other witnesses to the speech act. Robert Cialdini refers to these influences as social proofs. There are occasions when your behavior mirrors audience behavior. If a speaker asks a question, you are more inclined to provide verbal response if you are aware that others are inclined to do so. If the speaker says something amusing, you are more inclined to laugh outwardly if others are of the same disposition. Be aware, also, that these outward tendencies produced conjointly between you and others can also reflect favorably on the speaker in your post communication analysis.

Channels

All messages are received through the senses of sight, hearing, smell, feel, and taste. In the in-person situation a speaker may appeal to all of them much to his or her advantage. If the message appears on other channels, the respondents are handicapped because not all of the senses can be utilized. If a speech is recorded in a periodical like *Vital Speeches of the Day*, respondents have only the sense of sight. The smell, feel, and taste of newsprint is quite irrelevant and possibly distracting. If the speech is seen and heard on television, only those two senses can be used. If heard on the radio, only the one sense works for the respondents.

Quality, of course, can be achieved using channels other than the in-person situation. The author, in fact, uses three speeches from *Vital Speeches of the Day* in this book which he thought were very effective. You may disagree. There have been some quality speeches on television including President Reagan's speech at the dedication of the Statue of Liberty, although you may disagree. One of the finest speeches this author has ever heard was on the radio in 1959 when the late Dr. Thomas Dooley talked about his medical mission in Laos while visiting Seattle.

Often, the critic has only the artifact of a speech to work with. But the same dynamics of communication are at work as he or she studies it and many of the same elements of analysis and criticism are used.

The Occasion

The message must be appropriate to the speaker, the audience, and the occasion. Ayres and Miller simply refer to occasion as the purpose that brings a group together. [5] In the author's experience, most occasions are well-defined and most speeches presented on those occasions are appropriate.

You cannot ignore exceptions, however. If one has been asked to give a humorous speech, the purpose obviously is to make people laugh, but ideas intended to elicit laughter are sometimes uttered at the expense of a group particularly on the alert for direct or implied slurs. The author once found himself in this situation, and has since refused all invitations to present a "funny" speech. In the final analysis, you determine the appropriateness of the speech to the occasion, but you cannot ignore reactions of others in your post-communication review of events.

Summary

You have now been introduced to the elements of expression, your most tangible indication that the root system of the metaphorical tree of expression is alive and well. They consist of five components and were arranged in order of their importance. The *message* provides the nourishment. The *speaker* distributes the nourishment to the *audience* through well-defined *channels* always keeping in mind the appropriateness of the message to the *occasion*.

Footnotes (Chapter 2)

1. Raymond Ehrensberger, "An Experimental Study of the Relative Effectiveness of Certain Forms of Emphasis in Public Speaking," *Speech Monographs*, vol. 12 (1945), pp. 94–111.
2. Melvin Rader and Bertram Jessup, *Art and Human Values* (Englewood Cliffs, N.J.: Prentice-Hall, Inc., 1976), p. x.
3. As reported in Erwin Bettinghaus and Michael J. Cody, *Persuasive Communication*. 4th ed. (New York: Holt, Rinehart and Winston, 1987) p. 85.
4. Roderick P. Hart and Don M. Burks, "Rhetorical Sensitivity and Social Interaction," *Speech Monographs*, vol. 39 (1972), pp. 75–91.
5. Joe Ayres and Janice Miller, *Effective Public Speaking*. 2nd ed. (Dubuque: Wm. C. Brown, 1986), p. 21.

The Criticism
of Speeches

In Chapter One we looked at the Principles of Quality in Expression, and in Chapter Two how those principles were born out of The Elements of Expression. Now you are ready to go about describing and evaluating a particular communication event. Remember, you know what quality is when you observe it; now, can you articulate the reasons which led you to that conclusion?

Forms of Communication Events

Since communication events will occur in various packaging, we need to review what that packaging looks like. The most common form is the one you witness in-person. The event may be *informal* as in park bench conversation or formal as in public speaking. Both comprise the R^1–R^2 situation discussed in Chapter One where you, as a respondent, have the opportunity to act and react to the various elements of expression discussed in Chapter Two. You have the use of all five senses to discern what takes place, how and where, and a brain to interpret their significance to you. Criticism in the classroom is of this type.

A second form of a communication event occurs when you read a literary piece which may consist of a poem, an essay, or a speech. If it is a speech, since it has already been presented, it is a historical artifact which you may want to evaluate for its historical and rhetorical significance. Lincoln's Gettysburg Address is such a document, and after long study critics have judged it to be one of the great literary masterpieces of history. Martin Luther King's, "I Have a Dream," appears destined for immortality, as well. There are hundreds of such artifacts already uncovered by critics, and there hundreds more waiting for the pen of the critic. There are also many speeches less notable but nevertheless valuable for their intrinsic worth. As a critic, you have the opportunity of making judgments about that intrinsic worth.

What Is Criticism?

Criticism is the act of giving order to our perceptions and sensations about a speech.[1] You may perceive a speech as being "good," "bad," or "so, so." Persig writes that you are remarkably capable of this. Now, can you arrange your perceptions in an order that lends clarity and understanding to your original perception? The act of doing so is criticism.

Why Engage in Criticism?

Engaging in speech criticism serves a number of purposes. *First, it is a learning tool.* Your text is replete with rules which, if followed, will enable you to become a better communicator. In the act of criticism, you have to appropriate many of those rules which will help you determine which ones the speaker should or should not have used in the speech. Those which had a positive influence on your impressions will be the ones you will tend to remember and use in your own communication.

Second, it is an analytical tool. It forces you to think in a problem-solving manner. For example, suppose you have been asked to critique a speech you considered to be dull. It is not enough to say, "The speech was dull." You should describe the symptoms which led you to that conclusion. Having done that, you are in a position to make specific suggestions about how the speech could have been improved. What could the speaker have done differently to reduce predictability?

32

Third, it will help to improve your understanding of human nature. The social psychologist has formulated goals and values which govern much of our behavior. Through criticism, you improve your understanding of what goals and values seem to govern our attention and interest in the public speaking situation.

Fourth, your criticism may serve as a model for others to study. Although you are functioning as a critic, you are also conveying a message which may also be subjected to criticism by others. When you permit others to evaluate you, you develop further insights about criticism that you can build upon.

Fifth, speech criticism becomes another way of studying history. Through many centuries, critics have provided us with explanations and models of speeches which served as historical artifacts enabling us to better understand how the spoken word has both reflected and produced historical change.

Types of Criticism

For our purposes, let's place criticism into two categories: (1) *scholarly criticism*, and (2) *practical criticism*. Scholarly criticism, according to Bormann and Bormann, tends more to be an act of appreciation where the "fine points" of the art are examined critically as connoisseurs of any art are prone to want to do.[2] Publication of such articles tend to serve as building-blocks for the development of critical theory. Journals in speech communication contain an abundance of articles of this kind.

The criticism you should be thinking about is practical criticism. It is practical because it forces you to sharpen your senses of observation and your analytical abilities. It is practical because you develop insights about what goes into quality discourse. It is practical because, through your criticism, you can assist a speaker in evaluating his or her communicative efforts.

The Critical Method: Speeches You Witness

Now that you know what criticism is, why you should use it, what kinds of speeches there are, and the type of criticism you will engage in, you need to look at some methodological considerations for each of the forms of speeches. Assume, at this juncture, that you want to analyze and evaluate a formal speech of the type you might observe in a classroom setting. What follows are general suggestions which you will want to tailor to fit your own purposes. These suggestions will fall into four parts: (1) your behavior during the speech, (2) the procedure for analysis after the speech, (3) structuring your critique, and (4) presenting it.

Monitor Your Behavior During the Speech

There is a protocol that you will want to observe. In formal situations one person is verbalizing openly to many who are restrained in their verbal reactions. So, first, give the speaker a hearing by responding to his or her presence in a courteous manner. Be receptive. Second, respond within the confines of socially acceptable behavior. Remember, you are an equal participant in the act of communication because, without you and the other respondents, there would be no communication.

Next, you must be a *sensitive observer*. This means giving the speaker your *attention*. Attention may be thought of as a focus of perception leading to a readiness to respond. You may recall that Feature Three indicated that expression is of quality when it is marked by a readiness to respond. So, attention plays a key role in effective communication. By being attentive voluntarily, particularly in the early phases of a speech, you are giving an "artificial" interest to matters that do not have a natural interest for you. As the speech progresses, you may develop a natural interest and your attentiveness may become involuntary when understanding between you and the speaker becomes so intimate that the feelings, thoughts, and motives of one are readily incorporated by the other (Feature One). A sensitive observer also applies *listening skills* which would be impossible to use without attentiveness. Most texts devote considerable space to advising their readers on how to become better listeners. Last of all, *minimize note-taking* because you lose your communicative tie when you divert your mind to write an idea. When compelled to take notes, do so during those intervals of low energy output—virtually all speeches have them because sustained high energy output is extremely fatiguing for both respondents ravaging their mental capacities.

Assembling Your Reactions for the Post Speech Analysis

It is now time for you to reconstruct the speech not in a descriptive manner, but in accordance with your impressions—speaker behaviors which caused you to respond. Use description only to spur further impressions. A good place to begin is to start with your own personal, yet general, reaction. Chances are you are going to react in one of three different ways: you liked the speech, you did not like the speech, or you were indifferent toward the speech. Remember, you know quality when you observe it. Now ask yourself the question, why? Then relate it to (1) the degree to which you could relate to the presentation; or (2) the degree to which you could relate to the speaker. Once you have located one or more of the reasons, try to be more specific. Here is how you may proceed.

Step I. General Impression.
   A. "I liked the speech." (If was a satisfying experience)
   B. "I did not like the speech." (It was a waste of my time. In classroom criticism, you seldom hear this reaction because of its harshness)
   C. "I was indifferent." (It was not good and it was not bad. This may be the first symptom of a mediocre speech)

Step II. Specific reason(s) in support of the general impression

   A. "I liked the speech because . . ." (select one or more of the following reasons and add an additional one in the space provided)

   1. I agree with the speaker's ideas.
   2. The ideas were presented clearly and forcefully.
   3. I liked the speaker's persona.
   4. _____

   B. "I did not like the speech because . . ." (select one or more of the following reasons and add an additional one in the space provided)

   1. I disagree with the ideas.
   2. The ideas were not presented clearly and forcefully.
   3. I did not like the speaker's persona.
   4. _____

   C. "I was indifferent because . . ." (Select one or more of the following reasons and add an additional one in the space provided) The vast majority of classroom speeches fall into this category. They are what the author calls "mediocre."

   1. The ideas did not emerge clearly and forcefully.
   2. The speaker did not take maximum advantage of his or her persona.
   3. _____

Step III. Relate one or more of the reasons above to the elements of expression described in Chapter Two.

   A. "I liked the speech because:
   1. I agree with the speaker's ideas."
      a. I am willing to overlook other flaws.
   2. The ideas were presented clearly and forcefully."

a. The structure was clear.

b. The development or amplification was compelling.

c. The use of emphasis provided focus to important points.

d. Proportion was used effectively.

e. The strengths of the message stood out (weaknesses in the message were masked or de-emphasized).

f. There was a proper amount of redundancy.

3. I liked the speaker's persona.''

a. The speaker proved to be trustworthy.

b. The speaker displayed competence or expertise.

c. The speaker was dynamic.

d. The speaker was attractive.

e. I expect good things from this speaker.

f. I could easily relate to the speaker.

B. ''I did not like the speech because:

1. I disagree with the ideas.''

a. I cannot accept favorably what was said or how it was said.

2. The ideas were not presented clearly or forcefully.''

a. The structure was not clear.

b. The development or amplification lacked compellingness.

c. There was a lack of emphasis so I was unable to focus my attention on any particular point.

d. The speech was dull (disproportion).

e. Weaknesses in the message stood out.

f. There was little or no redundancy.

3. I did not like the speaker's persona.''
   a. The speaker is not trustworthy.
   b. The speaker lacked competence or expertise.
   c. The speaker was boring.
   d. The speaker could not talk away his or her face.
   e. I expected little, if anything, from this speaker.
   f. I could not relate to the speaker.
C. "I was indifferent because . . ." Use the checksheets in both A and B above because they will contain items that you liked and those you did not like.

Step IV. Relate your responses in Step III to the Principles of Quality in Expression.

Structuring Your Critique

Now you are prepared to structure your critique in accordance with the rules of outlining which appear in your text. Here is an example of what your basic structure might look like:

Subject Sentence: I liked the speech.

Main argument: The main ideas were presented clearly and forcefully.

Sub-argument: The development or amplification was compelling.

Example 1

Example 2

Sub-argument: The use of emphasis provided focus to important points.

Example 1

Example 2

Main argument: I liked the speaker's persona.

Sub-argument: The speaker displayed competence or expertise.

Example 1

Example 2

Sub-argument: I have grown to expect good things from this speaker.

Example 1 (your reaction to a previous speech given by this speaker)

Example 2 (your reaction to having been in other classes with the speaker)

Therefore, the strength of the speech was in the way the speaker reflected goodness (Feature Six) as revealed by his or her competence or expertise.

Now add this conclusion to your original Subject Sentence and you have the structure for a critique with the exception of introductory and concluding comments: "I liked the speech because the speaker reflected a goodness through his or her competence or expertise."

With a critique of this type, you are saying that the speaker's competence and expertise were the most compelling forces in the speech. It is likely that there were other desirable elements of expression present which did not become a focus of your perceptions. It is also likely that certain desirable elements of expression were not present, but their absence was masked or de-emphasized by more pleasing attributes.

The most challenging critiques to construct are with speeches which produced indifference, and they are by far the most numerous. With this kind of speech, the challenge is two-fold: (1) since it is missing many of the elements of effective expression, how can you keep your critique within manageable limits, and (2) how can you most effectively provide helpful suggestions for improvement?

Since you will find an abundance of missing elements of expression, focus on those which have common causes, and then propose solutions for those causes. For example, there will be a number of obvious symptoms indicating that the ideas were *not* presented clearly and forcefully (see Step III, A., 2. above). The most immediate cause obviously is lack of preparation. You may then propose that the speaker tighten the structure of the speech and, in addition, add examples of a compelling nature. You may want to stop there since the other symptoms relating to clarity and forcefulness probably stemmed from the anemia of logical structure and compelling examples.

Suppose the speaker displayed symptoms of shortcomings in the persona to a point where you question his or her competence or expertise (see Step III., A., 3. above). While the same lack of preparation might cause you to question his or her expertise, it might also suggest that the speaker simply did not devote enough time and thought to the preparation. You may want to suggest that he or she should provide some revelation that, indeed, materials for the speech were carefully gathered and structured without going into other determinants of the speaker's persona. One suggestion you might offer is to ask for sources of the information. The author recalls a recent speech delivered in class which was beautifully structured and included numerous authorities to back up the assertions. On the surface, it was a fine speech. Unfortunately, because three previous speeches given by this student were shallow, loosely constructed, void of compelling examples and expert testimony, and since no sources of the information were ever named in the speech, the author rightfully concluded that the student had plagiarized an entire article from a popular magazine. In that instance, the speaker's credibility was in question because he was too much out of character based on his past reputation. It may also be possible that the cause for your perceived lack of competence in the speaker may be due to reticence or stage fright. After all, that is the number one fear of the American people.[3] If you believe that to be the case, suggest portions of the text be reread and offer your own reassurances that the only thing the speaker has to fear "is fear itself."

With the mediocre speech, there is much construction to be done. It is better to start with a few helpful suggestions which can serve as a foundation for additional comments in subsequent speeches.

Presenting your Critique

You may present your critique in oral or written form. In either case, you already have it structured. If you present it in oral form, as in a speech, you are striving to achieve a positive effect by persuading your respondents that your point of view is a valid one. In your presentation, you want to conform to one or more of the principles discussed in Chapter One by employing various elements of expression discussed in Chapter Two. As a critic, you subject yourself to the very forces of criticism by your respondents that you used. If your critique is in written form, you need to remember that your recorded observations can be examined much more critically by the respondent. Aside from conforming to the rules of effective composition, strive to achieve a high degree of unity, coherence, and emphasis in your structure and limit you assertions to the examples you have available. Avoid statements you cannot support.

The Critical Method: Speeches You Read

Historical speeches serve as a window through which you can view the past and present. Sir Phillip Magnus, a biographer of the great British statesman of the eighteenth century, Edmund Burke, has written that his oratory "attained the furthest summit of political wisdom, and as literature his prose remains imperishable and unsurpassed."[4] Like "old soldiers," old speeches never die, they just fade-away only to be resurrected at a later time by in-

41

sightful political or rhetorical scholars who discern in them a significance that earlier critical scholars overlooked.[5]

Reading contemporary speeches has its advantages, as well. You can keep yourself informed on the most recent issues and events which may affect yours and others' lives. It is possible that the speeches contained in Appendix 2 of this book might influence your views on such common concerns as dieting and physical fitness. You can also study them as models of contemporary public speaking. Never forget the keys to quality in expression—theory you read in your text, practice, and models of speeches you witness and read.

It is ironic that in the current communications revolution, people are interacting to a much greater degree than ever before, but are recording fewer instances of that interaction. To some extent, the VCR has been of help, but the fact remains that the number of public speeches has proliferated in recent years while the reporting of those speeches in newspapers has become virtually non-existent. The author recently selected a random number of speeches from *Vital Speeches of the Day*, the one periodical dedicated to reporting "the important addresses of the recognized leaders of public opinion [which] constitute the best expression of contemporary thought in America. . . ." Each speech was delivered in one of the nation's largest cities. He then read the daily newspapers of each city on the day following each speech only to find that not a single speech, or even the occasion for the speech had been reported.

Nevertheless, some do exist in anthologies, *Vital Speeches of the Day*, sometimes in the *New York Times* or the *Christian Science Monitor*, often in bulletins distributed to stockholders or college alumni, in small town newspapers where a speech given locally is newsworthy, and probably in your text.

Your observation and analysis of recorded speeches are not as time bound as with the spoken word which requires that you receive instant impressions and compels you to record them before they evaporate from your recollection. You can examine written speeches carefully for organization, amplification, and style.

How then do you proceed? A good place to begin, after you have read it once or twice, is to divide your analysis into two divisions: (1) an internal analysis where you examine the speech itself, and (2) an external analysis where you look at circumstances leading to the speech and the effects of the speech, immediate and ultimate.

In your internal analysis, start with a question and look for the answer as you read the speech. Your question might be, "Do I like this speech?" You will most likely find the answer if you use the categories listed is Step III. If your question is, "Does this speaker abide by the same rhetorical principles in giving an informative speech as the authors of my text suggest?" You will then compare the speaker's ideas with the admonitions from the text. If you have done some external analysis of a historical speech, you might want to know how the speaker adapted to certain unique circumstances leading up to the speech. For example, Henry Grady, part owner and editor of the *Atlanta Constitution* was invited to speak to the New England Society at Delmonico's restaurant in New York City. So far there is nothing unusual about that circumstance, but you find that the event took place in 1886, with the wounds of the Civil War still fresh in the memories of all attending. Upon further research, you discover that the Republican Party, in its attempt to regain the presidency which it lost with the election of Grover Cleveland in 1886, was seeking to revive the heroic achievements of union forces during that war even to the point of having General William Tecumseh Sherman, who allegedly set the torch to Atlanta, precede Grady with a short speech starting with, "I have just returned from a bloody Civil War. . . ." You find from your research that northern newspapers praised the speech Grady presented that evening. With that extrinsic understanding, your question for intrinsic analysis might be, "How did Grady conciliate an antagonistic audience? Find the answer.

At this point, you should have a reasonably good idea about what constitutes extrinsic analysis. You are looking for background material relating to a particular speech. You may go to newspapers of the period, biographies, and histories. If you find a paucity of information from those sources, do not despair. You may want to propose that a particular speech, long neglected, deserves a prominent place in history by virtue of its substance.

Summary

In Chapter 3, you were introduced to the forms of communication events—those you witness and those you read. Following a brief definition of criticism, you were presented five good reasons for developing your own critical insights. After noting the two types of criticism, scholarly and practical, you were, finally, introduced to two practical methods which can serve to provide you with greater insight and analytical skill in evaluating those forms of communication events.

Footnotes (Chapter 3)

1. Herbert Read, *Art and Alienation* (N.Y.: The Viking Press, 1967), p. 64. I am borrowing freely from Read. Actually, he is concerned with the aim of the artist in producing an art object, but I could make a strong case for criticism being such an object.
2. Ernest G. Bormann and Nancy C. Bormann, *Speech Communication: A Comprehensive Approach*. 2nd ed. (New York: Harper & Row, 1977), p. 348.
3. Joe Ayres and Janice Miller, *Effective Public Speaking*. 2nd ed. (Dubuque, Ia.: Wm C. Brown, 1986), p. 21.

4. Sir Phillip Magnus, *Edmund Burke* (London: George Bell and Sons, 1891), p. 300.

5. Karlyn Kohrs Campbell, "Criticism: Ephemeral and Enduring," *The Speech Teacher*, vol. 23 (1974), pp. 9–14.

Recognizing Misused
Vocal Cues

In analyzing a speech, some of the most evasive symptoms to recognize and diagnose are the speaker's use and misuse of visual and vocal cues. In most instances, they work together. For example, if you note that a speaker has little bodily movement, he or she will probably have little flexibility of rate or pitch. The fact that you noted it, indicates that the speaker was emitting cues distracting you from other salient points of the presentation. If you were inattentive during a portion of the presentation, it is likely that the speaker was not using those cues effectively. Of the two, vocal cues tend to be the more pronounced. They are categorized under timing, pitch, loudness, and voice quality. Here are some of the common symptoms associated with each with their probable causes. The categories are taken from Grant Fairbank's, *Voice and Articulation Drillbook*. N.Y.: Harper and Brothers, 1940. The author notes the causes.

I. There is a problem of timing if:
> A. The speaker's rate is too rapid. The comfort level in public speaking is said to be about 175 words per minute [Ayres and Miller, 191]. If the speaker surpasses that, then discomfort might increase in the listener. The cause for this condition may be due to habit—the speaker "naturally" talks fast. It is more likely that the speaker is reading from a manuscript or has memorized the speech and is

not giving conscious thought to the ideas being expressed.

B. The speaker's rate is too slow. Discomfort will increase if the rate is considerably below 175 words per minute. This condition may also be due to habit, but that is rare with beginning speakers. It could be due to uncertainty, but usually other defects of timing, like poor phrasing, will emerge.

C. The speaker uses clipped or staccato phonations. Although this condition rarely occurs, it will appear consistently and is almost always attributable to habit. If it is interspersed in a speech, it is likely used for effect.

D. The speaker uses prolonged phonations, i.e. extends the vowels or diphthongs. It also rarely occurs, but when it does it might be attributable to dialect.

E. The speaker's timing is monotonous. That is a culprit which appears very often in speeches. Even though the speaker's rate may fall within your comfort zone, your mind can easily be lulled into somnolence by a constant dose of sameness. This condition is the result of habit coupled with the speaker's lack of concentration on the differing moods contained in the ideas.

F. The speaker may use faulty phrasing, obscuring true meaning. This condition occurs when the speaker either misuses the pause or fails to use it at all. This is due to uncertainty when the speaker is not sure of what ideas are to follow or how they should be phrased. Another common cause may be attributable to reading from a manuscript or memorization.

G. The speaker falls into time patterns. There may be variation of rate within each phrase, but the variation from phrase to phrase is the same. This is caused usually by failure to adapt ideas to the audience, producing monotony.

II. There is a problem of pitch if:
   A. The speaker's voice is too high or too low, causing discomfort within the listener. This is not a common problem with the vast majority of speakers.
   B. The speaker's pitch is inflexible. This condition occurs all too often! It reveals itself when the speaker fails to utilize those eighteen or so notes operating above and below the normal pitch level. It may be caused by habit, but more often is the result of the lack of attentiveness the speaker is paying to the ideas being communicated.
   C. The speaker uses pitch patterns. This is also a frequent occurrence. When the speaker is using variation in phrases but the variation becomes predictable among the phrases, them pitch patterns are evident. In this instance, the speaker is not aligning the ideas with the way the audience is reacting. It becomes monotonous to the listener by its predictability.

III. There is a problem of loudness if:
   A. The speaker is too loud. This condition occurs rarely. When it does, it is usually because the speaker is over-confident and is oblivious to the requirements of vocal adaptation.
   B. The speaker's voice is too soft. This condition can occur frequently. It tends to produce a tension in the listener who is striving uncomfortably hard to catch those weak vocalizations. It is usually caused by one or more things: shallow breathing, sometimes known as upper chest breathing, failure of the speaker to use all the resonators, and failure to adapt to the physical conditions.

C. The speaker's loudness level is monotonous. This is a frequent problem caused usually when the speaker fails to incorporate the mood being conveyed by the words.
D. The speaker is overly-flexible in the use of loudness. Seldom does this occur when the speaker goes from one extreme of loudness to the other.
E. The speaker uses loudness patterns. There is variation in the loudness levels but that variation becomes predictable. This usually occurs with experienced speakers whose ideas seem repetitive with each speech. Some observers have labelled this the "ministerial tone."

IV. The speaker has a problem with vocal quality if it is perceived as nasal, breathy, harsh, or hoarse. These symptoms are organic or functional requiring the assistance of a speech therapist. The one exception might occur when the speaker is breathy because of failure to control nervousness. This is a temporary condition and might even resolve itself before the speech is concluded.

Speeches for Analysis

Statement of John Forbes Kerry, Vietnam Veterans Against the War, to the Committee on Foreign Relations, United States Senate.

On April 22, 1971, 27 year old John Forbes Kerry, National Coordinator of Vietnam Veterans Against the War, testified before the Senate Foreign Relations Committee. His testimony was heard during a tumultuous week when hundreds of Vietnam veterans descended upon Washington to protest the war. That morning, 110 of his comrades were arrested for conducting an illegal protest on the steps of the Supreme Court. Later that day, A District Court judge overruled the arrest warrants and the veterans were set free. That evening, 700 vets and as many supporters staged a candlelight march from the Capitol to the White House back to the Capitol.

Kerry was born on December 11, 1943 in Denver, Colorado. He received his B.A. degree from Yale University in 1966. He was a naval lieutenant in Vietnam serving on gun boats plying the rivers in search of the enemy. While there, he earned the Silver Star, the Bronze Star with oak leaf cluster, and 3 purple hearts.

His testimony was covered by all three major networks, wire services, and numerous newspapers. Most would agree with an editorial in the *Sacramento Bee* which stated, "The Dilemma of American fighting men in Vietnam . . . was articulated eloquently before the US Senate Foreign Relations Committee by John Kerry. . . ."

In that same year, Kerry was author of a book titled, *The New Soldier*. He later resigned his commission and subsequently enrolled in law school at Boston College where he received his J.D. degree in 1976. From 1983–1985 he served as Lt. Governor of Massachusetts. In 1985, he was elected United States Senator.

Statement of John Kerry, Vietnam Veterans Against the War

Mr. Kerry. Thank you very much, Senator Fulbright, Senator Javits, Senator Symington, Senator Pell. I would like to say for the record, and also for the men behind me who are also wearing the uniforms and their medals, that my sitting here is really symbolic. I am not here as John Kerry. I am here as one member of the group of 1,000, which is a small representation of a very much larger group of veterans in this country, and were it possible for all of them to sit at this table they would be here and have the same kind of testimony.

I would simply like to speak in very general terms. I apologize if my statement is general because I received notification yesterday you would hear me and I am afraid because of the injunction I was up most of the night and haven't had a great deal of chance to prepare.

I would like to talk, representing all those veterans, and say that several months ago in Detroit, we had an investigation at which over 150 honorably discharged and many very highly decorated veterans testified to war crimes committed in Southeast Asia, not isolated incidents but crimes committed on a day-to-day basis with the full awareness of officers at all levels of command.

It is impossible to describe to you exactly what did happen in Detroit, the emotions in the room, the feelings of the men who were reliving their experiences in Vietnam, but they did. They relived the absolute horror of what this country, in a sense, made them do.

They told the stories at times they had personally raped, cut off ears, cut off heads, taped wires from portable telephones to human genitals and turned up the power, cut off limbs, blown up bodies, randomly shot at civilians, razed villages in fashion reminiscent of Genghis Khan, shot cattle and dogs for fun, poisoned food stocks, and generally ravaged the countryside of South Vietnam in addition to the normal ravage of war, and the normal and very particular ravaging which is done by the applied bombing power of this country.

We call this investigation the "Winter Soldier Investigation." The term "Winter Soldier" is a play on words of Thomas Paine in 1776 when he spoke of the Sunshine Patriot and summertime soldiers who deserted at Valley Forge because the going was rough.

We who have come here to Washington have come here because we feel we have to be winter soldiers now. We could come back to this country; we could be quiet; we could hold our silence; we could not tell what went on in Vietnam, but we feel because of what threatens this country, the fact that the crimes threaten it, not reds, and not red-coats but the crimes which we are committing that threaten it, that we have to speak out.

I would like to talk to you a little bit about what the result is of the feelings these men carry with them after coming back from Vietnam. The country doesn't know it yet, but it has created a monster, a monster in the form of millions of men who have been taught to deal and to trade in violence, and who are given the chance to die for the biggest nothing in history; men who have returned with a sense of anger and a sense of betrayal which no one has yet grasped.

As a veteran and one who feels this anger, I would like to talk about it. We are angry because we feel we have been used in the worst fashion by the administration of this country.

In 1970 at West Point, Vice President Agnew said "some glamorize the criminal misfits of society while our best men die in Asian rice paddies to preserve the freedom which most of those misfits abuse," and this was used as a rallying point for our effort in Vietnam.

But for us, as boys in Asia whom the country was supposed to support, his statement is a terrible distortion from which we can only draw a very deep sense of revulsion. Hence the anger of some of the men who are here in Washington today. It is a distortion because we in no way consider ourselves the best men of this country, because those he calls misfits were standing up for us in a way that nobody else in this country dared to, because so many who have died would have returned to this country to join the misfits in their efforts to ask for an immediate withdrawal from South Vietnam, because so many of those best men have returned as quadriplegics and amputees, and they lie forgotten in Veterans' Administration hospitals in this country which fly the flag which so many have chosen as their own personal symbol. And we cannot consider ourselves America's best men when we are ashamed of and hated what we were called on to do in Southeast Asia.

In our opinion, and from our experience, there is nothing in South Vietnam, nothing which could happen that realistically threatens the United States of

America. And to attempt to justify the loss of one American life in Vietnam, Cambodia, or Laos by linking such loss to the preservation of freedom, which those misfits supposedly abuse, is to us the height of criminal hypocrisy, and it is that kind of hypocrisy which we feel has torn this country apart.

We are probably much more angry than that and I don't want to go into the foreign policy aspects because I am outclassed here. I know that all of you talk about every possible alternative of getting out of Vietnam. We understand that. We know you have considered the seriousness of the aspects to the utmost level and I am not going to try to dwell on that, but I want to relate to you the feeling that many of the men who have returned to this country express because we are probably angriest about all that we were told about Vietnam and about the mystical war against communism.

We found that not only was it a civil war, an effort by a people who had for years been seeking their liberation from any colonial influence whatsoever, but also we found that the Vietnamese whom we had enthusiastically molded after our own image were hard put to take up the fight against the threat we were supposedly saving them from.

We found most people didn't even know the difference between communism and democracy. They only wanted to work in rice paddies without helicopters strafing them and bombs with napalm burning their villages and tearing their country apart. They wanted everything to do with the war, particularly with this foreign presence of the United States of America, to leave them alone in peace, and they practiced the art of survival by siding with whichever military force was present at a particular time, be it Vietcong, North Vietnamese, or American.

We found also that all too often American men were dying in those rice paddies for want of support from their allies. We saw first hand how money from American taxes was used for a corrupt dictatorial regime. We saw that many people in this country had a one-sided idea of who was kept free by our flag, as blacks provided the highest percentage of casualties. We saw Vietnam ravaged equally by American bombs as well as by search and destroy missions, as well as by Vietcong terrorism, and yet we listened while this country tried to blame all of the havoc on the Vietcong.

We rationalized destroying villages in order to same them. We saw America lose her sense of morality as she accepted very cooly a My Lai and refused to give up the image of American soldiers who hand out chocolate bars and chewing gum.

We learned the meaning of free fire zones, shooting anything that moves, and we watched while America placed a cheapness on the lives or orientals.

We watched the U.S. falsification of body counts, in fact the glorification of body counts. We listened while month after month we were told the back of the enemy was about to break. We fought using weapons against "oriental human beings," with quotation marks around that. We fought using weapons against those people which I do not believe this country would dream of using were we fighting in the European theater or let us say a non-third-world people theater, and so we watched while men charged up hills because a general said that hill has to be taken, and after losing one platoon or two platoons they marched away to leave the high for the reoccupation by the North Vietnamese because we watched pride allow the most unimportant of battles to be blown into extravaganzas, because we couldn't lose, and we couldn't retreat, and because it didn't matter how many American bodies were lost to prove that point. And so there were Hamburger Hills and Khe Sanhs and Hill 881's and Fire Base 6's and so many others.

Now we are told that the men who fought there must watch quietly while American lives are lost so that we can exercise the incredible arrogance of Vietnamizing the Vietnamese.

Each day—

[Applause.]

Each day to facilitate the process by which the United States washes her hands of Vietnam someone has to give up his life so that the United States doesn't have to admit something that the entire world already knows, so that we can't say that we have made a mistake. Someone has to die so that President Nixon won't be, and these are his words, "the first President to lose a war."

We are asking Americans to think about that because how do you ask a man to be the last man to die in Vietnam? How do you ask a man to be the last man to die for a mistake? But we are trying to do that, and we are doing it with thousands of rationalizations, and if you read carefully the President's last speech to the people of this country, you can see that he says, and says clearly:

But the issue, gentlemen,
the issue is communism,
and the question is whether
or not we will leave that
country to the Communists
or whether or not we will
try to give it hope to be a
free people.

But the point is they are not a free people now under us. They are not a free people, and we cannot fight communism all over the world, and I think we should have learned that lesson by now.

But the problem of veterans goes beyond this personal problem, because you think about a poster in this country with a picture of Uncle Sam and the picture says "I want you." And a young man comes out of high school and says, "That is fine. I am going to serve my country." And he goes to Vietnam and he shoots and he kills and he does his job or maybe he doesn't kill, maybe he just goes and he comes back, and when he gets back to this country he finds that he isn't really wanted, because the largest unemployment figure in the country—it varies depending on who you get it from, the VA Administration 15 percent, various other sources 22 percent. But the largest corps of unemployed in this country are veterans of this war, and of those veterans 33 percent of the unemployed are black. That means 1 out of every 10 of the Nation's unemployed is a veteran of Vietnam.

The hospitals across the country won't, or can't meet their demands. It is not a question of not trying. They don't have the appropriations. A man recently died after he had a tracheotomy in California, not because of the operation but because there weren't enough personnel to clean the mucous out of his tube and he suffocated to death.

Another young man just died in a New York VA hospital the other day. A friend of mine was lying in a bed two beds away and tried to help him, but he couldn't. He rang a bell and there was nobody there to service that man and so he died of convulsions.

I understand 57 percent of all those entering the VA hospitals talk about suicide. Some 27 percent have tried, and they try because they come back to this country and they have to face what they did in Vietnam, and then they come back and find the indifference of a country that doesn't really care, that doesn't really care.

Suddenly we are faced with a very sickening situation in this country, because there is no moral indignation and, if there is, it comes from people who are almost exhausted by their past indignations, and I know that many of them are sitting in front of me. The country seems to have lain down and shrugged off something as serious as Laos, just as we calmly shrugged off the loss of 700,000 lives in Pakistan, the so-called greatest disaster of all times.

But we are here as veterans to say we think we are in the midst of the greatest disaster of all times now because they are still dying over there, and not just Americans, Vietnamese, and we are rationalizing leaving that country so that those people can go on killing each other for years to come.

Americans seem to have accepted the idea that the war is winding down, at least for Americans, and they have also allowed the bodies which were once used by a President for statistics to prove that we were winning that war, to be used as evidence against a man who followed orders and who interpreted

56

those orders no differently than hundreds of other men in Vietnam.

We veterans can only look with amazement on the fact that this country has been unable to see there is absolutely no difference between ground troops and a helicopter crew, and yet people have accepted a differentiation fed them by the administration.

No ground troops are in Laos, so it is all right to kill Laotians by remote control. But believe me the helicopter crews fill the same body bags and they wreak the same kind of damage on the Vietnamese and Laotian countryside as anybody else, and the President is talking about allowing that to go on for many years to come. One can only ask if we will really be satisfied only when the troops march into Hanoi.

We are asking here in Washington for some action, action from the Congress of the United States of America which has the power to raise and maintain armies, and which by the Constitution also has the power to declare war.

We have come here, not to the President, because we believe that this body can be responsive to the will of the people, and we believe that the will of the people says that we should be out of Vietnam now.

We are here in Washington also to say that the problem of this war is not just a question of war and diplomacy. It is part and parcel of everything that we are trying as human beings to communicate to people in this country, the question of racism, which is rampant in the military, and so many other questions also, the use of weapons, the hypocrisy in our taking umbrage in the Geneva Conventions and using that as justification for a continuation of this war, when we are more guilty than any other body of violations of those Geneva Conventions, in the use of free fire zones, harassment interdiction fire, search and destroy missions, the bombings, the torture of prisoners, the killing of prisoners, accepted policy by many units in South Vietnam. That is what we are trying to say. It is part and parcel of everything.

An American Indian friend of mine who lives in the Indian Nation of Alcatraz put it to me very succinctly. He told me how as a boy on an Indian reservation he had watched television and he used to cheer the cowboys when they came in and shot the Indians, and then suddenly one day he stopped in Vietnam and he said "My God, I am doing to these people the very same thing that was done to my people." And he stopped. And that is what we are trying to say, that we think this thing has to end.

We are also here to ask, and we are here to ask vehemently, where are the leaders of our country? Where is the leadership? We are here to ask where are McNamara, Rostow, Bundy, Gilpatric and so many others. Where are they now that we, the men whom they sent off to war, have returned? These are commanders who have deserted their troops, and there is no more serious crime in the low of war. The Army says they never leave their wounded.

The Marines say they never leave even their dead. These men have left all the casualties and retreated behind a pious shield of public rectitude. They have left the real stuff of their reputations bleaching behind them in the sun in this country.

Finally, this administration has done us the ultimate dishonor. They have attempted to disown us and the sacrifice we made for this country. In their blindness and fear they have tried to deny that we are veterans or that we served in Nam. We do not need their testimony. Our own scars and stumps of limbs are witnesses enough for others and for ourselves.

We wish that a merciful God could wipe away our own memories of that service as easily as this administration has wiped their memories of us. But all that they have done and all that they can do by this denial is to make more clear than ever our own determination to undertake one last mission, to search out and destroy the last vestige of this barbaric war, to pacify our own hearts, to conquer the hate and the fear that have driven this country these last 10 years and more, and so when, in 30 years from now, our brothers go down the street without a leg, without an arm, or a face, and small boys ask why, we will be able to say "Vietnam" and not mean a desert, not a filthy obscene memory but mean instead the place where America finally turned and where soldiers like us helped it in the turning.

Thank you. [Applause.]

Analysis of John Kerry's testimony before the Senate Foreign Relations Committee

Author's note: This analysis is an exercise in practical criticism. I am interested in knowing why and how this speech affected me so that I may then convey to you a plausible argument as to why you, too, should be moved by it.

I liked the speech because John kerry became the Voice of my conscience. He stated eloquently what I would liked to have said. I lived through those years and observed many of the domestic side-effects of that war: I saw children of friends flee to Canada to avoid the draft; I witnessed student disorders on campus; I was bombarded with numerous instances of anti-establishment behavior, generally. I was led to ask questions millions of Americans were asking. "Why? What is to be the ultimate salvation we derive from all of this turmoil?" John Kerry supplied the one answer I was waiting to hear in the stirring epilogue of his testimony—our ultimate salvation is to get out:

> and so when, in 30 years from now, our brothers go down the street without a leg, without an arm, or a face, and small boys asks why, we will be able to say, 'Vietnam,' and not mean a desert, not a filthy obscene memory but mean instead the place where America finally turned and where soldiers like us helped it in the turning.

Who was this man who created such media attention immediately after his testimony? Few really knew, but he took only a few minutes to dispel the illusion that he was simply a rag-tag former military man in fatigues and sporting long hair. Soon, his credibility as a spokesman for a cause came to the surface. He was articulate considering "I was up most of the night and haven't had a great deal of chance to prepare." He was a man with a grasp of history through his allusion to Thomas Paine "in 1776 when he spoke of the Sunshine Patriot and summertime soldiers who deserted at Valley Forge because the going was rough."

He was a man sensitive to the feelings of his fellow veterans. He could transform their feelings of pain and anguish into words depicting the savagery of war with imagery so rich and so real:

> The country doesn't know it yet, but it has created a monster, a monster in the form of millions of men who have been taught to deal and to trade in violence, and who are given the chance to die for the biggest nothing in history; men who have returned with a sense of anger and a sense of betrayal which no one has yet grasped.

Each statement seemed to carry greater impact than the one before. If you were to ask me to identify the pattern of organization, I would reply, "I do not care about his pattern of organization, for whatever strengths or weaknesses it possessed, the forceful impact of his words supercede all other matters in my consciousness."

Did Kerry's testimony hasten the end to the war? Who can say definitively? There is little doubt in my mind that it was at least one of a hundred or perhaps a thousand indications of increasing discontent over a war we could not win. And it is likely that domestic discontent brought an end to that war.

The voice of John Forbes Kerry is still with us through this speech and many others since he has become a United States Senator. This one for me will always hold a special place.

We Dare to Hope for Our Children

Ronald Reagan

July 3, 1986

The text is taken from the *New York Times*, July 4, 1986

The text of this speech was issued by the White House in advance of its presentation by President Reagan on Governors Island before the relighting of the Statue of Liberty. Lee Iacocca introduced the President as "a man who made patriotism fashionable."

****

President and Madame Mitterrand, my fellow Americans. The iron workers from New York and New Jersey who came here to begin restoration work were at first puzzled and a bit put off to find foreign workers—craftsmen from France—arrive, too. Jean Wiart, the leader of the French workers, said his countrymen understood. After all, he asked, how would Frenchmen feel if Americans showed up to help restore the Eiffel Tower?

But as they came to know each other—these Frenchmen and Americans—affections grew; and so too did perspectives. The Americans were reminded that Miss Liberty, like the many millions she has welcomed to these shores, is originally of foreign birth—the gift of workers, farmers and shopkeepers who donated hundreds of thousands of francs to send her here.

The French workers, too, made discoveries. Monsieur Wiart, for example, normally lives in a 150-year-old cottage in a small French town, but for the last year he has been riding the subway through Brooklyn. A study in contrasts, he says; contrasts, indeed. But he has also told the newspapers that he and his countrymen learned something else at Liberty Island. For the first time, they worked in proximity with Americans of Jewish, black, Italian, Irish, Russian, Polish and Indian backgrounds. Fascinating, he said, to see different ethnic and national types work and live so well together.

It is especially fitting that this lesson should be relived and relearned here by Americans and Frenchmen. President Mitterrand, the French and American people have forged a special friendship over the course of two centuries.

61

In the 1700's, France was the midwife of our liberty. In two world wars, America stood with France as she fought for her life—and for civilization. So tonight, as we celebrate the friendship of our two nations, we also pray; may it ever be so. God bless America. Vive la France.

And yet, my fellow Americans, it is not only the friendship of two peoples but the friendship of all peoples that brings us here tonight. We celebrate something more than the restoration of this statue's physical grandeur. Another worker here, Scott Aronsen, a marble restorer, has put it well: "I grew up in Brooklyn and never went to the Statue of Liberty. But when I first walked in there to work, there's this feeling I can't describe. I thought about my grandfathers coming through here."

To millions returning home, especially from foreign wars, she was so special. A young World War I captain of artillery described how, on a troopship returning from France, even the most hard-bitten veteran had trouble blinking back the tears. And that is why tonight we celebrate Miss Liberty, this mother of exiles who lifts her light beside the golden door, this symbol of America, this vision of all that we are and wish to be.

We sometimes forget that even those who came here first to settle the new land were also strangers. Some have called it mysticism or romanticism, but I've always thought that a providential hand had something to do with the founding of this country. That God had His reasons for placing this land here between two great oceans to be found by a certain kind of people. That whatever corner of the world they came from, there would be in their hearts a fervent love of freedom and a special kind of courage, the courage to uproot themselves and their families, travel great distances to a foreign shore and build there a new world of peace and freedom. And hope.

Hope. Lincoln spoke about it. I told the story recently. He had just left the hometown he would never see again on his way to take up the duties of the Presidency and bring America through a terrible Civil War.

In Philadelphia he gave a speech in Independence Hall, where 85 years earlier the Declaration of Independence had been signed. His biographers tell us he spoke with great feeling, that he traced all his political ideas back to that document. He noted that much more had been achieved there than just independence from Great Britain. It was, he said, "hope to the world for all future time."

We, too, dare to hope. We dare to hope for our children; that they will always find here the lady of liberty in a land that is free. We dare to hope, too, that we will understand our work as Americans can never be said to be truly done until every man, woman and child shares in our gift—in our liberty—a light that, tonight, will shortly cast its glow upon her, as it has upon us for two centuries; keeping faith with a dream of long ago and . . . we dare to hope . . . guiding millions still to a future of peace and freedom.

Are You Fit for Life?

Michelle Nilsen
March 20, 1986
The text is reprinted by courtesy of the author.

Michelle Nilsen, a Communications major, presented this speech before a class in advanced public speaking. It was more than an assignment to her. It became her opportunity to testify on the merits of thoughtful food intake. It was a quality speech when she presented it; it is a quality speech now.

****

The first thing I want you to do is take out a piece of paper and write down everything that you put in your mouth yesterday. That's right, everything that you put in your mouth, and that includes liquids. Take your time, and if you're having trouble remembering, just go meal by meal. (pause) I hope this exercise has made you more conscience of your eating habits. You may be saying to yourself, "My gosh, I didn't know that I ate that much." Now I don't want you to feel guilty about what you ate yesterday. There's nothing that you can do about it now. So you might as well start off fresh today, without feeling guilty about yesterday.

Today I'm going to tell you how you can change your life for the better by changing your eating habits. ©FIT FOR LIFE does not require calorie counting. It is not a starvation diet. There are no drugs or powders. All of these other methods bring only a temporary change. FIT FOR LIFE brings about permanent results, because FIT FOR LIFE is not a diet. It is a different way to think about food. Now I don't know about you, but I have been on countless diets over the years, and anyone who has ever been on one knows why diets don't work. What is the one thing that you constantly think about while your dieting? You're thinking about all of the good food that you will get to eat when you lose those last ten pounds.

What is so completely new and different about this program is that it is not only what you eat that makes the difference, but it is of extreme importance when you eat and in what combinations. FIT

FOR LIFE is based on Natural Hygiene, which was originated in 1850. The basic principle behind Natural Hygiene is that the body is always striving to be healthy, and the body achieves this by constantly cleansing itself of waste material.

There are three cycles that the body goes through everyday and they are Elimination, Appropriation, and Assimilation.

The Elimination Cycle takes place from 4 a.m. until noon. This is when the body naturally rids itself of waste. This is the most important cycle in the FIT FOR LIFE program. During this time period you should eat nothing but fresh fruit and fruit juices. Anything else will halt the Elimination Cycle. Even if you decide not to follow the program for the rest of the day, it is essential that you have nothing but fruit until noon. You may have as much fresh fruit and fruit juice as you want. Melons promote the most weight loss, and bananas will help curb your craving for heavier, sugary foods. It is very important that you have your fruit on an empty stomach, never with or directly after a meal. The reason being that all fruits except for bananas take about a half hour to digest. Bananas take about forty-five minutes, but other foods take an hour or even longer. FIT FOR LIFE takes advantage of the digestive system process.

The Appropriation Cycle takes place from noon until eight at night. If you are hungry, this is the is the time to eat. Remember that digestion takes more energy than anything else you do. Everybody take out your list of food. Seventy percent of your food intake should be High Water Content Foods. And that does not mean just drinking water. Fruits and vegetables have high water content, anything else is a concentrated food. How much of the food on your list is High Water Content? I bet most of the food you ate yesterday was concentrated food. The world is composed of 70% water, as are our bodies. By stuffing ourselves with concentrated food, we are depriving ourselves from the water that we need so much. People who drink a lot of water, do so because they eat a great deal of concentrated foods, and they are constantly thirsty. Carnivorous animals eat animals that eat plants and fruit, that's where they get their High Water Content Food. The human body can only digest one concentrated food at a time. Any more than that and your system will be overloaded. That means no more steak and potatoes, chicken and noodles, cheese and bread, or cereal and milk. Properly combining foods does not mean that you can't have your favorites. You can have steak with vegetables or chicken with salad. Just remember to combine your meals right.

The Assimilation Cycle takes place from eight at night until four in the morning. This is the time to give your body a chance

66

to absorb and utilize all of the nutrients in the food you've eaten. No absorbtion will take place until the food has entered the intestine. A properly combined meal will be out of your stomach in three hours. It is important that you eat early, so that the food has left your stomach by bedtime.

(Using diagram B) Salad and raw vegetables take two hours to digest. A properly combined meal without flesh takes three hours to digest. A properly combined meal with flesh takes four hours to digest. And finally, an improperly combined meal will take eight hours, or even longer to digest. Remember an improperly combined meal is eating more than one concentrated food at a time.

(Using diagram C) This table shows you that you should eat fruits and vegetables earlier in the day. And meats and breads should be eaten toward the end of the day.

I usually have a banana and orange juice for breakfast. Then for lunch I have a properly combined sandwich, which consists of whole grain wheat bread, cucumbers, tomatoes, lettuce, with mayonnaise and mustard.

For dinner, I usually have a small salad, corn and a concentrated food like a baked potato or chicken. I'm usually satisfied with this amount of food, but I could eat more if I wanted to.

FIT FOR LIFE has changed the way that I think about food forever. I went off it over spring break, and paid for it. I had been off chemicals for over a month, and after abusing myself for a few days, I felt horrible. My whole attitude changed. I became irritable and impatient. I couldn't wait to detoxify my body when I got home. And I can see a real difference in my personality even after a few days.

Now that you've heard just a small part of the FIT FOR LIFE program, don't you think that you owe it to yourself to at least try it? Even if you are at your ideal weight, excluding chemicals from your diet can only enhance your life. I am challenging all of you to try to have nothing but fruit and fruit juices until noon. I guarantee that you will feel better both mentally and physically. I know I do.

Information taken from: FIT FOR LIFE by Harvey and Marilyn Diamond.

Diagram A:

ELIMINATION
4 a.m. to Noon
Body wastes and
food debris.

APPROPRIATION
Noon to 8 p.m.
Eating and
digestion.

ASSIMILATION
8 p.m. to 4 a.m.
Absorbtion
and use.

Diagram B:

FOOD	WAIT
Salad & raw vegetables	2 Hours
Properly combined meal without flesh	3 Hours
Properly combined meal with flesh	4 Hours
Improperly combined meal	8 Hours

A.M.

Diagram C:

Fresh Fruit & Fruit Juices
Fresh Vegetable Juice & Salad
Steamed Vegetables, Raw Nuts & Seeds
Grains, Breads, Potatoes, Legumes
Meat, Fish, Chicken, Dairy Products
P.M.

Corporate Fitness Programs Pay Off

Brenda W. Simonson
May 19, 1986
Reprinted by permission of *Vital Speeches of the Day*

Brenda W. Simonson is a Physical Fitness Consultant to Westwood Pharmaceuticals, Inc., a Subsidiary of Bristol-Myers Co. It was delivered to the Buffalo Chapter Administrative Management Society, Buffalo, New York. Note, particularly, its compellingness of detail.

****

The physical fitness boom of the 70's is getting its second wind in the 80's. The soft-sell of a decade ago is now the hard-sell by every self-proclaimed health freak that can chew sugarless gum and run at the same time. A fast arising awareness of health and fitness has overcome a generation who used to buy *real* sneakers—either Keds or Converse All-Stars. Now we have special shoes for each athletic event: walking shoes, running shoes, tennis shoes, aerobic dance shoes, dance shoes—much to the delight of the athletic apparel industry. This is good for the economy but it doesn't stop here.

In a nation where sophisticated health clubs offer every possible amenity from posh locker rooms with special phones to call in your take-out order, to tanning booths that enable you to age your skin at an alarmingly fast rate for only $3 per 15 minutes. What a deal! Today health and fitness can be bought for almost any price tag. From elite private clubs to backyard exercise classes, if you want fitness it's all there and you don't even have to look for it. In fact, there's no escaping the impact of this new wave of health conscious Americans.

Health clubs are standing on their heads to get you to join. The YMCA and Red Cross both offer special classes designed to improve your overall health—such as healthy back, nutrition and weight control, stress management and physical fitness training. Exercise classes for young and old are being taught in church basements, parking lots and backyards. Whether you lean toward the fancier private clubs, the mass appeal of the Y, or even your local community service groups, they all have the same purpose and goals—it's just the window dressing that's different. Anyway you package it, when administered by qualified personnel, achieving modest levels of health and fitness is the direction we want to go. For some it just takes longer. As a rule of thumb: For every year you haven't exercised, give yourself 2 months to get back into shape.

Where did all this enthusiasm get started? Surprisingly, we're a very unfit nation. In the early 1950's the Krauss-Weber physical fitness test for kids proved that in comparison to European children, we were a mess. From there the President's Council on Physical Fitness made giant strides in establishing appropriate levels of performance for a wide variety of sports. The council awards thousands of certificates for participation and achievement to all age groups through adulthood. In its prime, the President's Council was a real mover and a shaker in motivating kids to get out there and do something physical. Then the Olympics took over. Starting in 1968, the national pride resulting from the Olympians performance in Mexico City was contagious. The momentum carried on through the years has left a nation nearly gasping for air. The Olga Korbuts, Nadias, Bruce Jenners, Jim Ryans, and Mary Lou Rettons have paved the way for a nation to stand up and take a real hard look at their flabby thighs. Today athletic performance has become a high visibility media event. A few years ago, tennis players were banned from the court for wearing anything other than all white, now officials hold their breath waiting to see what calamity will take place next.

Has all this meant anything to the average couch potato who may someday buy his first running shoes? I think so. Viewing all this high level athletic performance has resulted in a trickle down effect and now 41 percent of Americans exercise or play sports regularly. Every week thousands of people *willingly* compete in:

• Triathlon events (swim, bike, run) over 1 million participants a year.

• Biathlons (biking and running).

• Marathons (26 + miles). The recent New York City Marathon involved 16,000 runners. Ultra marathons (50 + miles) with over 7,000 finishes.

• Iron man competition in Hawaii where you swim 2.2 miles in the ocean, bike 112 miles and then run a 26 mile marathon. There were 10,000 applications for 1200 available spaces.

Executives in Japan and Scandinavia long ago knew physical fitness made good corporate sense. Daily exercise, stretching and even yawning breaks are the norm. John H. Peterson of the National Cash Register Co. may have been the first American industrialist to see the benefits of on the job exercise. In 1944 he established morning and afternoon exercise breaks for his employees. He later expanded into recreational parks for his employees and their families.

The concept of physical fitness is changing and so is corporate America. The movement toward promoting healthy lifestyles in the workplace is picking up speed. The Association for Fitness in Business, formed in 1974 by two dozen industry fitness directors now has over 3500 members. Their recent annual meeting reported that corporate fitness centers originally established for white collar workers are now being expanded to serve an increasing number of blue collar workers who traditionally resisted the notion of exercise.

Most of the nation's $400 billion health-care bill goes to treat ailments resulting from potentially controllable problems like alcoholism, smoking, high cholesterol, hypertension and obesity. A top executive death from a heart attack can cost a company a half million dollars a year. As Emerson said: ''The first wealth is health'' or if you have your health, you have everything. That's why we are seeing thousands of firms from Fortune 500 companies to those with only a dozen employees are taking strides toward promoting fitness and safeguarding their employees' health. The popularity of corporate sponsored physical fitness and wellness programs, either with on or off-site facilities have made physical fitness an industry in itself.

Does fitness programming work?

When Fortune 500 companies each lose an average of $88 million a year to employee illness and over $100 million a year for employee medical coverage, you can bet health promotion in the workplace can be a terrific investment. The expense of an employee fitness center is minuscule next to the cost of unhealthy employees. To put this in perspective: The cost of the average size Christmas party for employees could equip and staff a modest wellness center for a year. The party is a one-night stand, a wellness center is a permanent fixture available for company-wide use everyday of the year. Does this sound like good business practice?

We at Westwood Pharmaceuticals here in Buffalo, are proud to know that our employee fitness program is one of the most advanced corporate programs in Western New York. Our participation rate among all employees is about five times what had been originally anticipated and enthusiasm for our special interest programs remains high. On a relatively modest budget we have been able to equip our wellness center with 16 exercise stations, not to mention the personal and professional attention each of our employees receives for training instruction.

71

But we are not alone. There are many companies which have turned to fitness and wellness programming to boost profits. For example:

Hospital Corporation of America pays participants 24¢ for each mile run or walked, each 1/4 mile swum or 4 miles biked.

Johnson & Johnson's "Live for Life" program awards health oriented prizes for adhering to good health practices (seat belts, work shops, smoke detectors, etc.)

The Scherer Lumber Co is proud to say "we have no sick pay, we have well pay." For each month a worker is not ill or late, they are given two extra hours of pay. At the end of the year, if you have missed no more than 3 days, you collect a $300 bonus.

SpeedCall Corp. gives $7 a week for not smoking at work. It's interesting to note that at the end of 4 years, smoking had declined by 65 percent and the number of insurance claims filed by quitters dropped 50 percent.

The U.S. Health Care Systems gives out 300 apples a day to employees in their smoke free facilities.

Control Data corporation reports that non-exercisers cost the company an extra $115 a year in health-care costs.

Lockheed Missiles and Space Company estimates that in five years it saved $1 million in life insurance costs through its wellness programs. Absenteeism is 60 percent lower and turn-over rate 13 percent lower among regular exercisers.

Dallas school teachers who enrolled in a fitness program took an average of 3 fewer sick days per year, savings of almost a half million a year in sub pay alone.

Marriot Hotel housekeepers do an early morning pool side aerobics class, the result has been fewer pulled muscles on the job.

Atco Properties pay $100 per pound lost during a 5 month period of time, $500 for stop smoking and $500 for regularly climbing stairs.

One of the pitfalls of setting goals with incentive rewards is that people get so caught up in trying to get a microwave oven that they might not get medical attention when they should. This is not good health practice. Erma Bombeck recently pointed out in her column that it's now unfashionable to be slowed down by what used to put us in bed for a week. Today, colds are dressed up and ignored, broken legs stop no one from flying coast to coast (you just leave a little extra time for limping), dental surgery is done in place of lunch and women plan their babies to be born around a long holiday weekend. It seems the incentive chase may be causing some stress of its own.

Overwhelmed by health and fitness myths and hype, oversimplification, mystification, half truth and lies, how does a company begin the groundwork for an employee wellness program?

The first thing is to realize that each and every corporate program has one thing in common—they began because someone like you, management or line worker, wanted to take the necessary steps to get it implemented. The next step is to determine whether or not the boss backs fitness. If there is interest and enthusiasm in the boardroom, you can cut through the red-tape and get your program started.

There are other ingredients for having a successful program:

1. Enthusiastic and well trained directors are more important than the fanciest equipment. They should have a working knowledge of exercise physiology, testing and prescription, principles of weight control and nutrition, injury prevention, basic business knowledge and good people skills. Studies have shown that you need 2 to 3 professional supervisors per 1,000 employees and 7 to 11 square feet of space per employee.

2. A planning committee comprised of fitness enthusiasts that represent all facets of the organization should be established. These people can help plan the annual schedule of wellness programs according to the needs and interests of fellow employees. These volunteers become role models and begin to take their own lifestyles more seriously, and in some cases, less seriously.

3. The program must offer a wide variety of exercise options to keep participants coming back. Equipment alone will only sustain interest for about seven weeks. Stretching and relaxation classes, beginners aerobics classes featuring low-impact exercise, classes for the very overweight, the over 50 crowd, nutrition counseling, dancing (square, round, ballroom) self-defense, etc. are all examples of what keeps your participants interested.

4. There should be incentives to draw the fence-sitters into the program. One company paid a dollar for every mile run, until the enthusiasm nearly broke the bank. A well publicized list of prizes spurs people on-ward and upward. Special exercise clothing with the company logo is another incentive. It is interesting to note that participation will be higher if companies fund most but not all the cost of participation. Employees who have no financial stake become lax.

5. The design of the fitness center should give workers a psychological change of pace by providing a non-work atmosphere of relaxation and well-being.

6. You must take into account the "culture" of the organization. In some companies, mixing management and other employees can be an incentive for everyone. In other places it might be best to have separate facilities.

7. Encouraging spouses to participate leads to support rather that resistance to the program.

8. The nuts and bolts of the content of the fitness center should be determined by the professional director. But here are a few guidelines;

a. The primary emphasis should be cardio-vascular conditioning (aerobics.) Treadmills, bikes, rowers, jump ropes, exercise classes, swimming, walking stairs all promote cardiovascular fitness.

b. Most facilities utilize a circuit training concept which maximizes participation and flow.

c. Employees should be screened based on personal health history and health risk appraisal.

d. A physical fitness profile should be administered prior to participation to determine work capacity, body composition, flexibility and muscular strength and endurance.

e. An individualized exercise program would then follow. Re-evaluation should take place every 4 to 6 months.

To be sure, this is not the last word in "how-to" develop a corporate fitness program. There are a number of trade secrets that have stimulated both large and small companies to re-examine where they are and where they could be with a commitment of a small amount of space, a little money and some creativity.

It is estimated that within the next five years, 25 percent of all major corporations in the United States will have established some sort of fitness programming. Indeed, corporate fitness programming has come of age. There's no doubt about it—healthy employees work more and cost less and that's why managers will embrace fitness, not as a fringe benefit, but as an integral part of a their regular personnel and health care policies. The message is clear—fitness means profits.

Will and Vision

Gerry Sikorski
June 1, 1986
Reprinted by permission of *Vital Speeches of the Day*

Gerry Sikorski is a United States Congressman from Minnesota. This is a Commencement speech delivered to the graduating class of Breckenridge High School, Breckenridge, Minnesota. It was meant to inspire, but notice the clarity of his ideas and the compellingness of his amplification material.

****

Graduates, parents and friends: I'm proud to be from Breckenridge and happy to be back today. And I'm really happy to see Ms. Linneman from my old days at Breckenridge High School. Did you know that she can predict the future? Time and again during my high school career, in library and study hall, Ms. Linneman would stop me in the halls and say, "SIKORSKI— I'VE BEEN WATCHING YOU. AND IF YOU DON'T CHANGE YOUR WAYS, YOU'RE GOING TO BE HERE 20 YEARS FROM NOW!" And Ms. Linneman was right. Here I am.

Writing a graduation speech is a real challenge. No graduation speaker I know has ever delivered a speech that any graduate has ever remembered 10 minutes after it ended. That's probably why so many Con-gressmen feel qualified to deliver them. I mentioned that to one of my colleagues in Washington last week, and she said, "Why go all the way back to Minnesota not to be listened to? Why don't you just write a letter to the President?"

Frankly, I don't remember who spoke at my graduation here 20 years ago. I don't remember a thing that he or she said. I do remember that it was hot as heck. The auditorium was packed and un-air-conditioned. And I remember thinking to myself: "HERE I AM SITTING INSIDE ON A 98 DEGREE DAY WITH A WOOL SUITE ON AND A GOWN OVER THAT. I SPENT HALF AN HOUR COMBING MY HAIR SO I COULD MESS IT UP WITH A HAT THAT LOOKS LIKE A GEOMETRY PROBLEM. AND I'M DOING ALL THIS BECAUSE

75

TODAY'S THE DAY I'M SHOWING THE WORLD HOW SMART I AM.''

Let's see. What else do I remember? I guess just that I was wearing a carnation that my Great Aunt Alice had crushed to death when she hugged me. And I remember that the kid sitting in front of me was wearing enough English Leather cologne to risk being shut down by the EPA. One of my classmates clipped his fingernails during the commencement address. Click. Click. Click.

But as I said, I don't remember the speaker. I suppose we were told that today was the first day of the rest of our lives. And I suppose we were told that we were about to enter "the golden door of opportunity." In 1966, the only door many young people were entering was the door to the draft board office—and the sign above it might just as well have said THIS WAY TO VIETNAM. It was the door from which too many did not return to finish the rest of their lives.

But you are a new generation and you don't need embroidered cliches any more than we did. I don't have to tell you that the world has changed in astounding ways during your lives. But it's amazing to think that when I went to B.H.S. we were reading the book "1984" as science fiction—while you read it as history.

The year 2000 was used as a science fiction writer's shorthand for some far-distant era. Today, the college class of 2000 is already in grade school. We are now as close to the 21st Century as we are to Vietnam and Watergate . . . and, I was going to say, to Richard Nixon. But I've just seen his smiling face on the cover of Newsweek. And I was reminded of the little girl in the TV ad for the new horror movie POLTERGEIST TWO, saying HEEE'S BAAAAAACK!

The re-emergence of Nixon got me to thinking that rather than spending these few minutes talking about changes—as exciting as they are—I want to talk with you about some things that stay the same. Countries change, technologies change, leaders change, but human nature and human challenge don't really change.

So to give you something to remember 10 minutes after graduation today, I did a little research. One of the best things about being a Congressman is that I meet a lot of exciting, successful people—religious, political, business and scientific leaders. So a few months ago, I started carrying a note pad around with me and asking those folks a question that went something like this:

"TELL ME THE MOST IMPORTANT THING YOU'VE LEARNED ABOUT LIFE AND YOURSELF AND PEOPLE SINCE YOU GRADUATED FROM HIGH SCHOOL?"

I want to pass along some of the best ones. Some you may agree with. Some you may think

76

are crazy. But I can almost guarantee you've heard every one of them from your parents. ("HEY NO GROANING THERE IN THE BACK ROWS!")

Number one is—BE ABSOLUTELY DETERMINED TO *ENJOY* WHAT YOU DO.

I've never met anybody who succeeded at something he or she hates. A news reporter interviewed Kenny O'Donnell, John Kennedy's friend and White House Chief of Staff some years ago. The interview was recorded shortly before O'Donnell's death, and you can tell by his voice that he wasn't well. But when the reporter asked him about the best part of his job with Kennedy, you could hear the energy coming back. He said:

"THE BEST PART WAS EVERY MINUTE OF EVERY DAY. I MEAN IT. I LOVED TO GO TO WORK EVERY DAY. BECAUSE I WAS DOING EXACTLY WHAT I WANTED TO DO ... WHERE I WANTED TO BE ... WORKING WITH WHO I WANTED TO BE WITH." Same with Kennedy.

Point number two—and almost everybody told me this in one way or another: DON'T BE AFRAID TO FAIL.

Lou Brock holds two baseball records: most stolen bases—and most times being thrown out trying to steal bases.

Babe Ruth holds two short season records: Most home runs—and most strike outs.

Columbus left Spain to find India. He failed. But he found America.

Lee Iacocca was fired by Ford Motor. Then he went to work and saved Chrysler. (Iacocca understood another great truth: Don't get mad. Get even.)

I'm not advising you to go out and fail. But when you fail at something—and you probably will—learn from it. An old saying goes: "The gifts are burdens. The burdens are gifts."

In 1972, I managed a congressional race and we lost. The next time, my candidate won.

In 1978, I ran for Congress and I lost. The next time I won.

Abe Lincoln lost five elections before he won the Presidency.

That brings me to another piece of good advice. NEVER GIVE UP ON ANYBODY. After all, Mark Twain pointed out 100 years ago that the only true and unredeemable criminal class in America is Congress.

"Never give up on anybody" was one of the favorite sayings of Minnesota's Hubert Humphrey. One of the last calls he made from his bed before he died was to Richard Nixon. They didn't agree on very much, but they shared a determination never to accept any defeat as final.

When you come back here for your 20th reunion, the success stories from this class of 1986 will amaze you. Don't be surprised if the fat kids with pimples come back looking more like Don Johnson or Christie

77

Brinkley. Don't be surprised if the kid who got the "D" in speech class comes back earning a quarter of a million dollars as a network newscaster. And don't be surprised if you come back happily married to the girl or guy you couldn't even stand to dance with at the prom.

And I hope you come back home often, because I can tell you from personal experience that when you face the toughest times in life, you have to be able to GET BACK TO YOUR ROOTS AND REMEMBER YOUR FUNDAMENTALS. That's the fourth point and those roots begin right here with your family and your community.

I'm proud to have my parents here in the audience today. Because when I talk about successful people, people who know a lot, they're on the list. My dad was a railroad worker. And for over 40 years, he worked on the bridges and buildings of Great Northern in the blistering heat of July and the terrible cold of January.

My mom took in laundry and gutted turkeys at the Swift plant. They had 8th grade educations. And now as they approach their 50th wedding anniversary, they don't have a lot of bucks. They're not written up in Who's Who. And Dan Rather doesn't interview them on the CBS Evening News. But that doesn't diminish the importance of their lives. They raised five kids and they raised us well. They overcame their problems. And they love each other. They taught us to work hard and care deeply. To suspect people on the make and still respect people who just can't make it. In the words of the song from the country-western band "Alabama:" "THEY DIDN'T KNOW NOTHING ABOUT A SILVER SPOON. BUT THEY KNEW A LOT ABOUT THE GOLDEN RULE." Thanks, mom and dad, for everything.

Speaking of getting back to fundamentals, I remember a Sunday twenty years ago when Coach Vince Lombardi watched his Green Bay Packers—the best team in football in the 60's—get absolutely slaughtered by the Chicago Bears—the worst team in football. (In those days, William "The Refrigerator" Perry was just a bouncing 100 pound baby boy).

Anyway, after that disastrous game, Lombardi got on the team bus. He was angry—really angry. And he shouted: "THIS TEAM IS GOING BACK TO FUNDAMENTALS. AND I MEAN REAL FUNDAMENTALS. AND WE'RE GOING TO START RIGHT NOW. THIS," he said holding up the ball, "IS A FOOTBALL." And from the back of the bus, player Max McGee shouted back: "HEY COACH . . . COULD YOU GO A LITTLE SLOWER? SOME OF THE GUYS AREN'T GETTING THIS ALL DOWN!"

Fifth, TRUST YOUR INSTINCTS. Your instincts come

from the fundamentals. So develop good ones and depend on them.

In one of his last songs, John Lennon wrote that "life is what happens to you while you're busy making other plans." And sometimes, your instincts are all you've got to tell you you're moving in the right direction when everyone else is telling you you're going crazy.

Sometimes your instincts will tell you to break the rules. A couple of years ago, a small New York City advertising firm landed the account for NIKE shoes and sportswear. And they developed an ad campaign that everybody in the advertising industry predicted would be a total disaster. Because they broke all the rules. They produced a series of billboard and magazine ads with people wearing Nike products. But the people didn't look like the glamorous and sophisticated sorts who lounge around. They were runners— dirty, sweaty, exhausted—finishing a race and looking like they were about to throw up. And the word NIKE appeared on the ad— not in huge letters at the top—but in tiny, almost unreadable letters at the bottom. The ad campaign failed miserably—right? Wrong! It boosted Nike sales by 25 percent and helped make the firm one of the fastest growing, most successful advertising agencies in the world. That happened because those people trusted their instincts. But there's more to it:

Trust your instincts and never give up on yourself. That's the sixth point.

Just a few years ago, a young writer named John Kennedy O'Toole won a Pulitzer Prize for his book "A Confederacy of Dunces." It was not a history of Congress or an analysis of this Administration's farm policy. Rather, it is hailed as one of the great humorous works of the 20th Century. But O'Toole never knew he'd won the Pulitzer prize, because after having his manuscript rejected by 17 publishers, he took his own life.

His mother found the hand-typed manuscript when she was going through his things and she took it to publishers. The rest is history and the lesson is clear. Never, never give up on yourself—and never ever underestimate the power of others who love you and will never give up on you either.

When you make the commitment never to give up on yourself, you come to understand the last bit of advice I want to leave you with today. And it's simply that in your own life, and in the life of your country—ONE PERSON— YOU—CAN MAKE A PROFOUND AND LASTING DIFFERENCE.

It's easy to diminish our own importance. The mathematicians tell us that in terms of size, our significance is infinitesimal. A map of the universe that we know of would be 80 miles long. On that map, our galaxy would take up one 8 1/2 by 11 sheet. Our solar system would be a molecule on that sheet. And earth would be a speck on the molecule. The astronauts tell us that as they observe Earth from outer space, they don't think about Star Wars defense systems. Instead they see Earth as one vulnerable ship Gallactica, riding through a cold and dangerous universe as the lone outpost of humanity.

We are the stewards of human progress on this planet. Human progress is a chain, and every generation forges a little piece of it. You've heard the old expression that a chain is only as strong as its weakest link. My challenge to you today is to do what you can in your own lives to strengthen your link and thereby hand down a stronger chain to the next generation.

That's what President Kennedy had in mind when he told us that from now on, every generation will have the capacity to make theirs the best in the history of the world—or the last. For from those to whom much is given, much is expected. Now, the great unfinished tasks are being passed into your hands. And your obligation is to carry on for those who have gone before and after you. Truly: "If it is to be . . . It is up to you."

IF JUSTICE IS FINALLY TO BE GAINED FOR THE OP-PRESSED, it will be because your generation gives us people like Martin Luther King—who faced guns and police dogs be-cause he believed that injustice *anywhere* is a threat to justice *everywhere.*

It will be because your generation gives us people like Lech Walesa—who stood before God and the world and insisted on basic human rights for Polish workers and farmers; Jacabo Timmerman—who had just toured the Argentinian jail cell where he was tortured—but this time as a free man; Cory Aquino, who with yellow dress, tenacity and right, brought down a mighty and corrupt regime in the Phil-lipines.

IF THE HUNGRY ARE TO BE FED, it will be because your generation gives the world people as committed as Harry Chapin, who gave the last years of his short life, not to the riches he could gain for himself as a singer, but instead to raising millions of dollars to help feed the hungry. Harry died on the way to one of those concerts. But just a few days ago, millions joined "Hands Across America" to help finish what he began.

IF OUR CHILDREN ARE TO HAVE CLEAN AIR, GREEN TREES AND CLEAN WATER, it will be because your generation gives the world more people like Lois Gibson—who risked her life to expose what the chemical companies had done at Love Canal.

AND IF WE ARE TO GET WASTEFUL SPENDING CHECKED, it will be because your generation gives us more people with the courage of Ernie Fitzgerald. He sacrificed a career at the Pentagon by telling what he knew about a $3 billion cost overrun for the C58 Transport Plane almost 20 years ago. Since then, he's been harassed, threatened and demoted. But he's still talking. And he's giving others the courage to talk about $5000 toilet seats and generals and admirals spending tax dollars like drunken ensigns and privates.

In short, WHEN OUR TWO TRILLION DOLLAR NATIONAL DEBT IS FINALLY PAID, WHEN RURAL AMERICA IS FINALLY SAVED, WHEN THE ARMS RACE IS ENDED BEFORE THE HUMAN RACE IS ENDED, it will be because your generation and those who come after you take to heart what Robert Kennedy told students just your age in South Africa 20 years ago:

He said:

"EACH TIME A HUMAN BEING STANDS UP FOR AN IDEA . . . OR ACTS TO IMPROVE THE LOT OF OTHERS . . . OR STRIKES OUT AGAINST INJUSTICE . . . HE OR SHE SENDS OUT A TINY RIPPLE OF HOPE. IN CROSSING EACH OTHER FROM A MILLION DIFFERENT CENTERS OF ENERGY AND DARING, THOSE RIPPLES BUILD A MIGHTY CURRENT WHICH CAN SWEEP DOWN THE MOST TER-RIBLE WALLS OF OPPRES-SION AND INJUSTICE.''

I submit that you do not represent America's last generation— but America's best generation. You will not find all the answers. The poet Carl Sandburg once wrote that as a nation, America is more the seeker than finder—ever seeking its way through storms and dreams.

And as you seek your way for yourself and America, you will have the tools you need. All the tools Americans have needed to overcome world wars, great depressions, and terrible natural disasters:

• The values of a just society.
• The strength of a revolutionary democracy.
• The power of a free economy.
• The muscle of a skilled workforce.
• The talents of an educated people.

But that's not enough. As the Book of Proverbs tell us, ''where there is no vision, the people perish.'' We need the vision of a restless people.

Our vision for ourselves and our country should be as John Steinbeck described it:

"I SEE US . . . NOT IN THE SETTING SUN OF A DARK NIGHT OF DESPAIR AHEAD. I SEE US IN THE CRIMSON LIGHT OF A RISING SUN, FRESH FROM THE BURNING, CREATIVE HAND OF GOD. I SEE GREAT DAYS AHEAD. GREAT DAYS MADE POS-

SIBLE BY MEN AND WOMEN OF WILL AND VISION." You are those men and women of will and vision. So go to work and carry on.

Thank you very much.

Trade Conflicts
Ichiro Hattori
November 19, 1985
Reprinted by permission of *Vital Speeches of the Day*

Ichiro Hattori is President of Seiko Instruments and Electronics. He delivered this speech to the Los Angeles Area Chamber of Commerce, Business Outlook Conference, Los Angeles, California. American businesses have long believed that the tremendous trade imbalance between the United states and Japan has been due in a large part to prohibitive tariffs the Japanese have placed on American imports, while Japanese products shipped to the United States can maintain their competitive pricing. Mr. Hattori is undoubtedly facing an audience dubious, at best, about how effectively he can reconcile their beliefs.

****

This year, issues over trade conflicts between Japan and the United States attracted both the highest political priority and the continuous attention of the press. The wave of protectionism gained momentum in Washington with the Senate's Resolution of March 28 criticizing the Japanese.

In response, Japan has taken several steps toward opening her market. how open is it? I cannot answer this question in quantitative terms. For the best answer, however, I would like to borrow the words of Mr. Mike Mansfield, American Ambassador to Japan and of Yoshio Okawara, former Japanese Ambassador to Washington. In an interview with *The Washington Post*, Ambassador Mansfield said the "Japanese market is not as closed as most Americans believe it is, and the American market is not as open as Americans believe." This perhaps is one sided. You might even say that Ambassador Mansfield has become Japanese.

Commenting on the Mansfield remark, Ambassador Okawara writes that "the Japanese market, too, is not as open yet as most Japanese believe." I think the words of the two ambassadors combined offer a fair description of the present status of the Japanese market, and the perception of people thereof on both sides of the Pacific.

In the perception of most Americans, the liberalization measures, if they have been effective, must be translated into increased sales of American products in the Japanese market and into the reduction of the trade imbalance between our countries.

A huge trade imbalance still exists between us. However, we should not overlook gradual changes. The Japanese share of the U.S. external trade deficit has been declining. In 1982, one-half of the U.S. trade deficit was attributable to Japan. It was about one-third in 1983 and still less in 1984. Japan is the second largest importer of American products, next only to Canada. Contrary to popular belief, about one-half of Japanese imports from the United States comprise so-called manufactured goods; and the value of such manufactured goods increased by nearly 8 percent in 1984 from the previous year.

I know Americans are getting impatient, but people do not turn around so quickly. After all, Japanese have only recently found out that their domestic products are as good as, or better than imported products.

For a long time, Japanese used to prefer imported goods to domestically manufactured goods. It took Japanese consumers more than twenty years to rid their products of the notorious image of "cheap but inferior". This is understandable because most of the products were, indeed, not only "cheap but inferior" but at the same time often "inferior but expensive".

We have to understand that in the nature of things it takes a long time to alter consumer psychology. It does not happen overnight.

Taking that into consideration, I would like to say that the market-opening measures for manufactured products have begun to take effect.

The effectiveness of the market-opening measures, however, are obscured by the overwhelming amount of the trade imbalance. As long as the imbalance exists, the improvement scarcely reaches the eyes and ears of Americans.

But, I would like to assure you that the efforts for opening up the market will be continuously pursued by the Japanese Government and will be supported by our business community. There are differences of opinion between the business community and government ministries regarding the extent and speed of the liberalization. It seems to me, however, that the differences more often that not promoted liberalization. Nothing new, after all, can be expected where there is just one opinion.

These efforts to liberalize the market should be further pursued, and we Japanese shall be glad to listen to recommendations or constructive criticism from foreign countries as to how it should be done.

Yet, as we all know, some of the criticism these days is hardly constructive. The notion that Japanese trade policies are unfair is alarming indeed. For example, Americans attribute the loss of jobs in the United States to Japanese trade practices and this notion has become the central tenet of the promoters of protectionism.

This situation is dangerous, firstly, because it promotes protectionism which is bad for everyone and, secondly, because it jeopardized the otherwise sound bilateral relationship between our two countries. This is a situation with which we Japanese cannot live comfortably. And I do want to make some observations now on this situation.

In my opinion, those people who criticize Japan often lack knowledge of vital facts and make shortcuts in their thinking process. They conclude that Japan must be engaged in unfair trade practices simply because Japan has accumulated a large amount of trade surplus from the United States. But, they are overlooking many important facts about themselves.

If they would turn around from time to time and see what is happening in the United States they would see that, just as Japanese companies are beginning to come to the United States for manufacturing, American companies are increasing their offshore purchases.

It is common knowledge that Japanese color television manufacturers have set up production facilities in the United States and, recently, Korean manufacturers have started to do the same. But not much is made of the fact that American TV makers are producing almost all of their sets overseas. Calling it "offshore production," they import televisions from places like Mexico, Taiwan, and Singapore, where they are produced either through O.E.M. arrangements or in plants under their direct control.

The same phenomenon is now beginning to take place in automobile manufacturing. The newspapers report that, one after another, Japanese car makers are setting up production facilities in the United States.

An American automobile company, meanwhile, is building a major plant in Mexico, and substantial numbers of small American-brand cars are now manufactured by Japanese and other foreign automobile manufacturers. We now are seeing American-made Japanese cars competing in the United States with foreign-made American cars.

In other words, American consumers will be asked to make a choice between a SONY TV made in the U.S. and a Zenith TV made in foreign countries, or a Honda car made in the U.S. and a Dodge car made in Japan.

Another development along the same line is the news that American high-tech firms are moving to Mexico and other off-shore sites to lower their labor costs. Mexico has severe restrictions on foreign investment, which has only been permitted with the participation of domestic capital. But, apparently, this requirement has been waived for IBM, which will own 100 percent of the plant it builds. Already the bulk of the components that go into American personal computers are imported. Just recently, *Business Week* reported that even IBM's personal computers include overseas-made parts that account for 70 percent of the manufacturing cost.

It should come as no surprise that the biggest exporter of Japanese-built computers is IBM Japan. In 1984, IBM Japan exported just under one billion dollars of products, amounting to 30 percent of its total sales. An American semiconductor manufacturer, meanwhile, has built a modern plant in Japan and is producing chips on a vast scale, both for sale in Japan and for export to the United States. These exports by American affiliates now constitute a not insignificant portion of Japan's exports. In 1984, exports to the United States by subsidiaries of American companies in Japan amounted to about two billion dollars; and exports to the United States by Japanese companies under OEM arrangements amounted to five billion dollars.

Some people criticize the Japanese government for subsidizing R&D expenses of private companies. This practice, of course, is not a monopoly of the Japanese. Nearly 50 percent of all R&D expenses in the United States is paid for by public funds. The government of the United States provides a large and guaranteed market for companies in defense businesses. This is a look-alike, only on a far greater scale, of the Japanese practice of developing the telecommunication industry through the N.T.T. organization.

This may all be fine, but a sad trend in the United States is that no sooner do valuable new technologies start to create jobs within the United States than the work is snatched away and shipped abroad.

Sadder still is the fact that such freedom of shifting production abroad is mainly enjoyed by large multinational companies. Medium and small-sized companies in conventional manufacturing businesses have neither the ready access to government sponsored R&D results nor the facilities for going offshore for production. Foreign governments do not grant special concessions to small companies, while they are happy to extend them to multinational companies like IBM. In my opinion, this discrepancy, if allowed to continue, will eventually weaken the strength of the American industry as a whole.

I would like to make one more point here. *The Economist*, in its July 6 issue, reported that, on a per capita basis, the Japanese bought $481 worth of American goods (including products made by subsidiaries of U.S. companies in Japan), while Americans spent only $287 on Japanese goods (including local production by Japanese firms in the United States).

Considering all of this, the Senate Resolution of March 28 this year criticizing Japan was, indeed, an extraordinary show. Not a single vote was cast against it. It was even more extraordinary in view of the fact that even the declaration of World War II was not carried unanimously. Free expression of minority opinion has always been the best part of a democracy. If the resolution should be interpreted to mean anything beyond a show of the Senate's muscles to the White House, then we must conclude either that the Senate completely lacked knowledge of the facts or that something, indeed, went wrong with the democratic conscience of this country.

To decide what is fair and what is unfair in international trade is no easy matter. When there is controversy between people or companies within a nation, the court of justice can decide who us unfair. But, when there is controversy between nations, they usually cannot agree on a court to judge their dispute, because a nation, especially a powerful one, cannot recede from what it believes to be its own rights.

Because America rightly believes that it is the superpower of the Western World, Americans often assume that they know the rules of the game. But, the role of America in international trade is at least a little more complicated and carries a greater responsibility than the role of the New York Yacht Club in the America's Cup Race. The rules of international trade should not be established by one nation's subjective definition of justice, but should be agreed upon by mutual consent with full knowledge of the facts that are available.

I have nothing against overseas production of American companies *per se*. I am not about to say what American companies should be doing. Japanese companies, too, shifted production to Asian nations where wages were lower. This helps expand the economy in real terms for the world. Nor do I want to make an issue out of Japan bashers who turn international economic problems into domestic political problems. But, let us be clear and agree at least on one principle; that nobody can be his own judge and, in international trade, the rules of the game by which to decide who is fair or unfair should be agreed upon by mutual consent.

The United States and Japan share many values. By any standard both are very democratic countries and both have a free market economy. Yet, there are also differences. The United States is a country of immigrants and Japan is a country with the most homogeneous people in the world. While the majority of the U.S. population originated from European cultures steeped in the tradition of Christianity, Japanese culture is entirely non-Christian.

There is little doubt that it will take time to create mutual consent on the concept of fairness in international trade between two different cultures. Many Americans assert that the size of the imbalance must reflect unfair practices. This assertion comes from their experience because for a long time American businessmen worked conscientiously, and there was never a country like Japan to deal with in those days.

The Japanese people strongly feel that Japan should be given more time for the change and adjustment. They, too, believe that they have been working conscientiously. While realizing the need for change, Japanese wonder if it is not unfair for other nations to force a rapid change that might cause great damage and pain to particular segments of their industry, such as, for instance, the lumber and plywood industries.

Thus, the need of deepening mutual understanding about fair practices in trade is urgently needed. But, in the meantime, we should never change our view that it is always bad to engage in protectionism. If the United States adopts protectionism against Japan, it may reduce its trade deficit with Japan temporarily at the cost of the American consumers. But, that does not mean a true expansion to either economy.

This is much like pushing one side of a balloon so that it can bulge on the other side. In Japan we call it gambling between father and son. There is nothing genuine about it. True opportunities of expansion for our manufacturing industries can only come from developing countries. These are the countries where future consumers are to be found. Some of them are just coming into the stage where protectionist economic policies may be abandoned. If we now embark on protective economic policies ourselves, how then can we ask those countries to open their doors to us when their people are ready to import our products. No nation can be so unabashed as to use such a double standard in its trade practices.

Coming back to our own problems, let me put forth my own outlook for our bilateral trade relations, particularly for the time after the new values for the yen and the dollar become at least stabilized, if not established.

The new rate at 200 yen plus to one dollar was welcomed by many circles in Japan. This will give at least temporary relief to the trade negotiators of both governments. The new rate, however, has made a far greater impact on Japanese industry than just buying time. This is a transformation of management thinking—a renewed conviction that Japanese industry must become more international in its manufacturing as well as in its financing facilities.

Already, Japanese companies are increasing their investment in the United States, and the circumstances for creating successful manufacturing ventures in the United States have been well documented elsewhere. In my opinion, a stronger yen and the increase of Japanese manufacturing in the United States will produce and ultimately eliminate the trade imbalance.

It cannot happen next year, but I am certain that it will happen in three to four years time. The key will be increased Japanese manufacturing in the United States and this will be facilitated by other trends:

1. In Japan, employment in the manufacturing industries will be cut back. The activity level of manufacturing is related to the export activity and, hence, to the exchange rate. A strong yen combined with persistent threats of protectionism will keep Japanese companies shifting their production to the United States, thereby reducing employment in Japan.

2. Short-term capital outflow from Japan will also be reduced simply because there will not be so much surplus to be invested. Instead, Japanese companies will intensify their efforts to raise capital overseas.

3. In the United States, Japanese investment will halt the offshore shift manufacturing. It is likely that more new jobs in the U.S. manufacturing industry will be created by Japanese companies than anyone else.

All of this will change the present U.S.-Japan relationship in a very favorable direction, and if we can have but 3 years to allow these factors to do their job, today's cries for protectionism will have become a bad dream hardly ever talked about any longer.

Finally, to conclude my talk, I would like to touch once more on a point I made earlier, which is that Americans must understand that to expand the world economy in real terms, we must have more people participate in consumption. There is a limit to the expansion of the consumer population in North America, Europe and Japan.

Increased consumption in the remainder of the world, however, cannot occur with war and violence. To expand the consumer population, a continuing peace in larger areas of the world is and will always be the vital factor. I am afraid, however, that peaceful countries and the number of their people are today less than ten years ago. Countries like Cambodia, Vietnam, Iran, Afghanistan and Lebanon have been lost as consumer markets as a result of war or other violence. The market for consumer products in Latin America and many African countries have been diminished in size for one reason or another. We have a shrinking world in terms of the size of the consumer market. How we can turn this situation around and expand the size of the world consumer market is the crux of the problem which we all face today.

To address this problem is a mission truly worthy of the United States, the superpower of the Western World, and perhaps of Japan, also. Japan bashing and creating protective barriers may satisfy the emotion of the moment, but is neither a lasting nor a meaningful solution.

I thank you.

Index

Amplification, 18
Analysis of John Kerry's
    testimony, 59
Aristotle, 27
Attention, 34
Attractiveness, 25
Audience, The, 27
Ayres, Joe, 29, 44

Bettinghaus, Erwin, 15, 30
Bormann, Ernest G. and
    Nancy C., 33
Burke, Edmund, 41
Burks, Don M., 27

Campbell, Karlyn Kohrs, 45
Channels, 28
Cialdini, Robert, 12, 28
Cody, Michael H., 15, 30
Competence, 25
Conversational model, 1
Credibility, Components of,
    12, 25–27
Critical method in
    speeches you read, 41–44
    speeches you witness,
      34–41
Criticism
    defined, 32
    purposes of, 32
    types of, 33
Critique, presenting your, 41

De-emphasis, 23
Dress, 12, 26
Dynamism, 25

Ehrensberger, Ray, 19
Empathy, 4
Emphasis, 18
    verbal, 18
    nonverbal, 19
Energy, 21–23

Features of quality, 3
    summarized, 14

Goodness in the speaker, 12
    factors of goodness, 12
Grady, Henry, 43

Hart, Roderick P., 27
Heron, Woodburn, 5

Ideas, where to place, 20
Inner depths of the mind, 8

Jessup, Bertram, 21

Kilpatrick, James L., 4

Lasting impression, 13
Loudness, problems of, 49

Magnus, Sir Phillip, 41
Malik, Charles, 5
Masking, 23
Miller, Janice, 29, 44
Monotony, 6
Motivated expression, 10–11

Name recognition, 12, 26

Occasion, 29
Organizational structure, 17

Phaedrus, 2
Pirsig, Robert M., 2

Pitch, problems of, 49
Proportion, 20
    energy in, 21–23

Quality
    defined, 2

Rader, Melvin, 21
Read, Herbert, 44
Readiness to respond, 7
Redundancy, 23
Roosevelt, Franklin, 13

Similarity, 13, 27
Speaker, The, 24
"Starving artist" theory, 9

Timing, problems of, 47
Trustworthiness, 25

Unpredictability,
    in composition and
      delivery, 5

Vital Speeches of the Day,
    28, 42
Vocal quality, problems of,
    50